MARK

The Gospel of Action

MARK

The Gospel of Action

By

RALPH EARLE

MOODY PRESS • CHICAGO

Library of Congress Catalog Card Number: 71-104824

ISBN: 0-8024-2041-9

Printed in the United States of America

To
Bill and Emily Pfeiffer,
Denise, Scott and Mark,
in whose hospitable
country home this book
was written

CONTENTS

CHAPTER   PAGE

Introduction   9

Outline   13

I.   The Period of Preparation (1:1-13)   15

II.   The Galilean Ministry (1:14—9:50)   18

III. The Perean Ministry (10:1-52)   83

IV.   Passion Week (11:1—15:47)   93

V.   The Resurrection (16:1-20)   125

Bibliography   127

INTRODUCTION

The gospel according to Mark is the shortest of the four gospels. It is also generally considered to be the earliest in time of writing.

Its brevity is due to the fact that it contains less of the teachings of Jesus than the other three. Mark's gospel is primarily the gospel of action. About two out of three verses begin with "And." In fact, a glance down through the first chapter will show that most of the verses begin this way. As someone has well observed, "His narrative runs." Over forty times we find "immediately," "straightway," or "forthwith"—all translations of the same Greek word. It might be said that, while Matthew and Luke furnish us with colorslides of the life of Christ and John presents a studied portrait, Mark gives us a moving picture of the Master's ministry.

This gospel of action has only one long discourse of Jesus—the so-called Olivet Discourse found in Mark 13, Matthew 24—25 and Luke 21. It is a significant fact that this one lengthy discourse deals with the second coming. Before Christ went to the cross, He was concerned to assure His disciples that He was coming again.

Again, Mark has only four of the parables of Jesus. In contrast, Matthew records fifteen parables and Luke nineteen. (This computation is based on Trench's total of thirty parables; some harmonies list almost twice as many, including short parabolic statements.)

9

But, while this gospel of action has just one long discourse, it records eighteen miracles performed by Jesus. The much longer gospels of Matthew and Luke have only twenty each. Early church tradition says that Mark wrote his gospel in Rome. The Romans liked action. So Mark presents Jesus as the mighty Conqueror—over disease, death, demons, and the elements of nature.

Mark also portrays Jesus as Servant. In line with this two-fold presentation we find no genealogy in this gospel. Servants do not parade their pedigrees. Nor were the Romans concerned about the ancestry of their great conquerors. What they wanted was action. The question was not Where did he come from? but What can he do? Matthew, writing for Jews, begins his gospel with a Jewish genealogy of Jesus, tracing his lineage from Abraham down through David. The origin of the Messiah was of supreme importance to the Jews. Luke furnished for his Greek readers a genealogy of Jesus that followed his ancestry back to Adam. John begins with what might be called the spiritual genealogy of Jesus; He was the preexistent, eternal Son of God. All of this was irrelevant to the Roman mind.

In the first two chapters of Matthew and Luke we also find what are known as the Infancy Narratives—stories of the birth and childhood of Jesus. None of this is found in Mark's gospel. With only a short account of the ministry of John the Baptist and a brief description of the baptism and temptation of Jesus, Mark plunges immediately into the public ministry of Jesus in the fourteenth verse of his first chapter. In contrast to the 13 verses of introduction in Mark we find 76 verses in Matthew and 183 in Luke! In both latter gospels the public ministry does not begin until the fourth chapter.

Mark's is also the most *vivid* of the gospels. Vincent notes that it is "preeminently the pictorial Gospel." Though the entire gospel is shorter than the other three, Mark's account of a particular incident in the life of Christ is often longer than that found in Matthew or Luke. This is because he adds vivid details. For example, He gives special attention to the looks (3:5) and gestures (10:16) of Jesus. All these we catch in this moving picture of Jesus' ministry.

A third feature of Mark's gospel—after rapid action and vivid detail—is picturesque description. In connection with the feeding of the five thousand, for instance, Mark alone mentions the green grass. He also says that the people sat down in companies as "flower beds" (see p. 60).

The early church Fathers are unanimous in saying that Mark's gospel gives us the preaching of Peter. The whole gospel fits his personality. This apostle was a man of action, of the outdoors. When he saw the crowd of people in their colorful oriental garments reclining in orderly groups on the green grass of the hillside, they looked to him like flower beds.

The tradition of the early church uniformly assigns the writing of this gospel to John Mark. He is first mentioned in Acts 12:12. When Peter was released from prison he went to the home of "Mary the mother of John, whose surname was Mark." John was his Jewish name; Mark (Marcus) his Roman name. As with many other Jews in the Roman Empire (e.g., Saul, Paul) he probably had both names from birth.

When Barnabas and Saul returned from their so-called famine visit to Jerusalem (Ac 11:27-30), they took John Mark along with them (Ac 12:25). He accompanied them on their first journey as their attendant but left the missionary party at Perga (Ac 13:5, 13). For this reason Paul refused to take him along on the second missionary journey (Ac 15:36-41). But later the apostle mentions him as his companion in Rome (Col 4:10; Phile 24). Finally, in 2 Timothy 4:11, Paul writes: "Take Mark, and bring him with thee: for he is profitable to me for the ministry"—or, "for serving me." The young man who had failed so pathetically in the beginning at last made good. This is still an encouragement to those who are plagued with their failures of the past. Anyone who will can stage a full comeback.

When was Mark's gospel written? The traditional date was in the 50s, though a majority of scholars today prefers the date A.D. 65-70. In any case, it was written within forty years (perhaps twenty-five) of the events it records. Under the inspiration of the Holy Spirit Mark gives us an authentic account of Jesus' ministry.

OUTLINE

I. The Period of Preparation (1:1-13)

II. The Galilean Ministry (1:14–9:50)

III. The Perean Ministry (10:1-52)

IV. Passion Week (11:1–15:47)

V. The Resurrection (16:1-20)

I

THE PERIOD OF PREPARATION
1:1-13

1. The Title (1:1). This first verse may be taken as a heading for the entire book or as referring only to the ministry of John the Baptist. Many of the early church Fathers preferred the latter. Modern commentators are divided in their opinions about this.

The word *gospel* (*euangelion*) means "good news." So we might translate the title: "The beginning of the glad tidings about Jesus Christ, the Son of God." The good news of salvation begins with the historical fact of Christ's life, death and resurrection. Christianity is not some nebulous philosophy; it is firmly rooted in history. It is more than an ethical system; it is a way of salvation. Someone has well said that the gospel is "not good advice but good news." It is the glad tidings that what we could not do for ourselves Christ has done for us on the cross.

2. The Ministry of John the Baptist (1:2-8). All the gospels present the events connected with Jesus' life and ministry as a fulfillment of Old Testament prophecy. So here Mark quotes Malachi 3:1 (v. 2) and Isaiah 40:3 (v. 3) as predicting the work of the forerunner of the Messiah. John was to prepare the way for Jesus. Recent versions have "Isaiah the prophet" instead of "the prophets" in verse 2 (see ASV) in accordance with the oldest Greek manuscripts. The main emphasis was on the quotation from Isaiah, as a comparison with Matthew and Luke will show. His prophecy was the best loved and most widely read by devout Jews in Jesus' time, as the large number of Isaiah manuscripts in the collection of Dead Sea Scrolls from Qumran would seem to indicate.

John told the people to repent, in preparation for the coming of the Messiah. Those who repented he baptized in the Jordan River, as they were "confessing their sins" (v. 5). *Repentance* (v. 4) means literally a change of mind, that is, a changed attitude toward God, sin, and oneself. The Baptist declared that while he baptized *with water*, the coming one would baptize *with the Holy Ghost* (v. 8). Water baptism, practiced by Judaism and other religions, is important. But the baptism with the Holy Spirit, which only Christ can give, is all-important.

John the Baptist was a rugged prophet from the wilderness. He was clothed in the rough sackcloth made of camel's hair. He ate locusts (similar to grasshoppers) and wild bees' honey (v. 6). He was a fearless preacher like Elijah of old.

3. The Baptism of Jesus (1:9-11). Large crowds were coming to hear John preach and to be baptized by him (v. 5). But one day a unique figure appeared on the banks of the Jordan. It was John's relative, Jesus. He had come from His hometown of Nazareth, which was situated to the northwest in central Galilee. He did not need to repent, for He had never sinned. But as the representative man who was to die for our sins He had to identify Himself with mankind and submit to the repentance-baptism (cf. Mt 3:13-15).

As Jesus came up out of the water, He saw the heavens *opened*. Mark alone uses here the strong word *schizō* (cf. schism), which means "split apart." This is an example of the vivid language of Peter.

It is at the baptism of Jesus that we have the first clear

revelation of the Trinity. The Holy Spirit descended as a dove on Jesus, and the voice of the Father proclaimed: "Thou art my beloved Son." Here the three Persons are clearly distinguished. The deity of Jesus is a basic, vital part of the gospel. Without a divine Redeemer there is no salvation from sin. Christianity is the only religion which claims an eternally divine Founder (cf. 1:1). When we surrender the deity of Jesus, we relegate Christianity to a lower place as simply one of the many religions of the world.

4. The Temptation of Jesus (1:12-13). Again we note the word *immediately* (cf. Introduction). All three synoptic gospels place the temptation of Jesus right after His baptism.

Once more we find Mark using a stronger word than Matthew and Luke. He says that the Spirit *driveth* Jesus into the wilderness. There on the rocky, barren hillsides of the Wilderness of Judea, Christ was tempted for forty days by Satan. Matthew and Luke each record three distinct temptations of Jesus. Mark gives only a brief summary statement of this crucial experience in Christ's life.

It was necessary that Jesus' public baptism should be followed by a private period of testing. He must be tempted in all points as we are, that He might be our merciful and faithful High Priest (Heb 2:17-18; 4:14-16).

II

THE GALILEAN MINISTRY
1:14—9:50

1. The Beginning of Jesus' Ministry (1:14-15). The arrest and imprisonment of John the Baptist marked the commencement of Jesus' great Galilean ministry. He did not wish to run in competition with His forerunner. But when John's voice was silenced, a greater Preacher appeared. He was "preaching [lit., proclaiming or heralding] the gospel of the kingdom of God." This kingdom had now come in the person of the Messiah. The command was "Repent ye, and believe the gospel." To the Baptist's preaching of repentance there was added the new note of believing the gospel, the good news of salvation.

2. The Call of the Four Fishermen (1:16-20). John 1:35-42 shows that these four men formerly had been disciples of John the Baptist. But when he pointed out Jesus as the Lamb of God, they followed Him to His abode. This poses no conflict with the synoptic account. In the latter we have the call of these four fishermen to full-time service. They were asked to leave their business on the lake and follow Jesus as *fishers of men* (v. 17). They "straightway forsook their nets, and followed him" (v. 18). Their obedience was immediate and complete. It should be noted that forsaking must always precede following. We cannot follow Jesus until we are willing to forsake our own plans and wishes.

As usual, Mark adds a little item of interest. He says that James and John left their father Zebedee "in the ship with the hired servants" (v. 20). The aging father was not left bereft and helpless by the departure of his sons. The hired servants would enable him to carry on the prosperous business of the family.

Christ calls busy men. The ministry is no place for idlers and quitters. The New Testament portrays these four apostles as active workers before the Master called them to His service.

3. The Cure of a Demoniac at Capernaum (1:21-28). Jesus chose Capernaum as the headquarters of His great Galilean ministry. This commercial city was on the main road of caravan traffic between Egypt and Damascus. While the obscure mountain village of Nazareth was a better place for Christ to live in as a child, His public ministry needed the wider perspective of a busy city.

On the Sabbath day Jesus entered the synagogue and began to teach (v. 21). The people were astonished at His doctrine (better, "teaching"). The scribes were in the habit of quoting the opinions of various rabbis, but Jesus spoke with direct divine *authority* (v. 22).

In the synagogue that Saturday morning was a man with an *unclean spirit* (v. 23)—Mark's favorite designation for a demon. The spirit recognized who and what Jesus was. He suddenly cried out, identifying Him as "the Holy One of God" (v. 24), that is, the Messiah. Christ rebuked the unclean spirit and commanded him to "hold thy peace [lit., "Be muzzled!"] and come out of him" (v. 25).

Why did Jesus refuse the testimony of this demon to His deity? Probably He objected to the source. Also it was not yet time for Him to be proclaimed publicly as Messiah. Such an announcement might precipitate a political revolt against Rome.

Cruelly the unclean spirit convulsed its victim and screamed out in anger and frustration. But it had to obey the divine command and so came out (v. 26). The amazed onlookers exclaimed, literally, "What is this? A new teaching!" (v. 27). The report of this incident quickly spread throughout Galilee (v. 28). This is the first miracle of Jesus recorded by Mark and Luke. Matthew omits it.

4. The Healing of Peter's Mother-in-Law ((1:29-31). After the synagogue service Jesus and His disciples went home for dinner at Peter's house. (This was the big meal of the day, as the Jews did not ordinarily eat before going to worship.) They found Peter's mother-in-law in bed with a sudden raging fever (v. 30). But the guest of honor became the physician of the hour. The woman was healed instantly and served the dinner. One can imagine the joy with which she waited on Jesus. The whole incident shows the Master's love for people and for the home.

5. A Sunset Healing Service (1:32-34). The Jewish Sabbath lasted from sunset Friday to sunset Saturday. During this time no one could carry any burden. So, as soon as the sun went down Saturday evening, the people began bringing those who were sick or demon-possessed to the door of Peter's home. The exciting news of what had happened that morning in the synagogue had spread throughout the city. Doubtless some had also heard how Jesus had healed Peter's mother-in-law. Anxious friends and relatives could hardly wait for the sun to set so that they might bring the needy ones to this miracle-worker in their midst. It seemed to Peter that "all the city" was gathered in front of his house (v. 33).

Jesus healed many who were afflicted with "divers [various] diseases and cast out many devils" (v. 34). The word *devils* should be *demons*. The Greek is careful to distinguish between *diabolos* (devil) and *daimonion* (demon). The former is always singular in the New Testament when applied to Satan, for there is only one devil. The latter is usually plural, as here, for there are many demons (evil spirits). It is incorrect to speak of "devils," though many British scholars still do it.

Again we are told that the demons *knew him* but that He did not permit them to testify to His identity. This was His settled policy.

6. A Sunrise Prayer Time (1:35-39). The Greek text has three adverbs (very, early, by night) to emphasize how early it was when Jesus rose and went out of the city to a solitary place to pray. He had just had an extremely busy day in Capernaum. Now he needed spiritual renewal, more than a long sleep, as well as fresh guidance from His Father concerning which direction to take. If Jesus felt this need for prayer, how much more should we!

Peter (Simon) and the other disciples "followed after him" (v. 36)—literally, "hunted him down." Evidently He was in such a secluded place they had some difficulty in finding Him. When they did discover where He was, they informed Him that everybody was looking for Him (v. 37). There were many sick people who had failed to get to Jesus the night before but anticipated reaching Him in the morning. To their dismay they found that He had left town.

The disciples doubtless were disappointed when Jesus answered that He must go into the adjoining country towns, rather than back into the city. His primary ministry was not to heal the sick but to preach the gospel. Many people had not yet heard; He must go to them. It was for this purpose that He "came . . . forth" (v. 38). Came forth from where? Some scholars answer, "Capernaum." But the parallel in Luke 4:43, "for therefore am I sent," seems clearly to indicate heaven. Christ came forth from the Father to proclaim the gospel.

Redeeming the souls of men was more important than healing their bodies.

Verse 39 makes a summary statement about Jesus' synagogue ministry "throughout all Galilee." It was primarily a preaching tour, though He also cast out demons.

7. The Cleansing of a Leper (1:40-45). Lepers were considered unclean and so were required to keep a safe distance from their fellow Jews so that they would not contaminate them ceremonially. But this leper came hurrying to Jesus for help. Since he sensed no opposition from the Master, he continued until he knelt right in front of Him, so near that Jesus could touch him (v. 41). This is a good illustration of the truth of the promise, "Him that cometh to me I will in no wise cast out" (Jn 6:37).

The leper had more faith in Christ's power than in His love. He said, "If thou wilt, thou canst make me clean" (v. 40). The Master was "moved with compassion." This phrase, found frequently in the gospels, has the participle in the aorist tense, so it is more adequately translated "gripped with compassion." This was Jesus' immediate reaction when confronted with human need.

In a spontaneous gesture of divine love Christ reached out with His hand and touched the leper, thereby contracting ceremonial defilement in the eyes of the Pharisees and Sadducees. But instead divine power annulled the contamination and effected a cure. All the Master had to say was, "I will; be thou clean." His love was equal to His power. In fact, the two cannot be separated, for divine love is the greatest power in the universe. As soon as Jesus spoke in love, the leper was instantly healed. Since leprosy was considered an uncleanness, the word used to describe the cure is *cleansed* (v. 42).

At this stage in His ministry Jesus was seeking to avoid publicity. The multitudes thronging around Him to be healed would hinder His evangelistic ministry. So He sternly *charged* (v. 43)—a strong term in Greek—the man not to tell anyone about his cure but to report it to the priests, that they might officially pronounce him clean (see Lev 14:1-32). Instead the man told everybody about it. The unwanted result took place. Jesus could not even enter the city during the day but had to remain outside in unpopulated areas. Still the crowds kept thronging to Him.

8. The Healing of a Paralytic (2:1-12). At the completion of His tour of Galilee (1:39), Christ returned to Capernaum. "It was noised that he was in the house" (v. 1) is better translated "It was heard, 'He is at home.'" As would be expected, immediately a crowd gathered, and soon it was impossible to reach the door of Peter's home. But Jesus was now doing what He always wished to do: "he preached the word unto them" (v. 2).

There was one needy man in Capernaum who had failed to get in on the famous sunset healing service (1:32-34). We can imagine that, when he heard about it, he cried out in disappointment, "Why didn't you take me to Him?" Probably his relatives assured him that they would do so the next day. But with morning came the disquieting news, "The Master is gone." His hopes blasted, the poor paralytic had to remain in his misery. ("One sick of the palsy" [v. 3] is one word in Greek, *paralyticon,* and should be translated "a paralytic.")

Now came the exciting news, "He is at home." *Four* men— only Mark gives this interesting detail—each took hold of a corner of the padded quilt on which the helpless paralytic was lying, and using it as a stretcher they started for Peter's house.

But when they arrived they could not get near Jesus because of "the press" (v. 4)—not newspaper opposition (!), but simply "the crowd." Nothing daunted, these four persevering friends laboriously carried the paralytic up the outside stairway onto the flat roof of the one-story home. Here they literally "unroofed the roof." That is, they dug down through the hard-packed dirt. Then they broke up the tiles (cf. Lk 5:19). When they had made a large enough hole, they lowered the paralytic on his pallet right down in front of Jesus.

When Christ saw their faith—the faith of the four and also probably of the paralytic—He said, "Son, thy sins be forgiven thee" (v. 5). The Greek says, "Your sins are [or, have been] forgiven you." It was not a wish; it was an accomplished fact.

Two things may be deduced from this. The first is that the man's greatest need was not the healing of his body but the saving of his soul. The second is that the man's paralysis may have been brought on in part by a massive guilt complex. He must first be relieved of his burden of sin before healing could take place. The Jewish Talmud contains an old saying of the rabbis: "No one gets up from his sickbed until all his sins are forgiven" (*Ned.* 41*a*).

As usual, there were some scribes (Pharisees) sitting there, "reasoning in their hearts" (v. 6). They were saying to themselves, "Why does this man talk this way? He blasphemes! [so reads the best Greek text] Who can forgive sins but God only?" (v. 7).

When Jesus "perceived in his spirit" (v. 8) their inner thoughts, He challenged them. Which was easier, to tell the paralytic his sins were forgiven or to tell him to get up and walk? (v. 9). To prove that "the Son of man hath power on earth to forgive sins" (v. 10), Jesus turned to the paralytic and commanded him to rise, take up his pallet, and go home (v. 11). The helpless victim *immediately* stood to his feet, threw his padded quilt over his shoulder, and walked out, leaving an astonished crowd behind.

The point of this incident now becomes clear. The scribes held that a man could not be healed until all his sins had been forgiven. The paralytic had been obviously healed; no one could deny it. But according to the rabbinical saying, that meant that his sins must first have been forgiven. How then could these religious rulers deny Jesus' power to forgive sins?

One other item might be noted. What is the answer to Jesus' twofold question of verse 9? Probably it would be easier *to say* "Your sins are forgiven," since no one could prove that they were not forgiven. The second command, "Arise . . . and walk," would put Jesus "on the spot." Actually, of course, the one was just as easy as the other for the Son of God.

9. The Call of Levi (2:13-14). Again Jesus went out of the city and walked along the shore of the Lake of Galilee. It doubtless seemed a relief to get away from the stuffy atmosphere of pharisaic criticism and breathe the refreshing air from off the water. But still the crowds thronged around Him. As always, He gladly spent His energies in teaching them.

As He walked by the lake, He saw a man named Levi sitting at the *receipt of custom* (v. 14). This is one word in Greek. It has been variously translated "tax office," "tollhouse," or "customhouse." A tollhouse on the highway from Damascus perhaps does not fit with the mention of the seaside (v. 13). It may have been a place where import and export duties were received on goods transported across the lake from one province to another, or where a tax was collected on fish caught in the lake. In that event, Levi would have been well acquainted with the four fishermen-disciples. Probably the simplest translation is the more general one, "tax office." At any rate, Levi was a tax collector. He is better known to us by his other name, Matthew, which perhaps was his Christian surname. He is probably to be identified with the author of the first gospel. When Jesus spoke those magic words, *Follow me,* Matthew immediately rose and followed.

10. The Feast in Levi's House (2:15-17). The new disciple invited his Master to his home for dinner. Luke specifically says, "Levi made him a great feast in his own house" (Lk 5:29). Jesus "sat at meat" (v. 15)—literally, "was reclining [at the table]." The Greeks and Romans had the custom of reclining on cushioned couches around the table while eating, and the well-to-do Jews had copied this leisurely practice.

Many publicans (more accurately, "tax collectors") and sinners (Jews who were careless about observing the Law meticulously) were reclining at the table with Jesus and His disciples, for *many* of these people followed him. It seems rather obvious that Matthew planned this feast with a three-fold purpose: to honor his Master, to say farewell to his old associates, and to bring them into contact with Christ.

The Pharisees (v. 16) are specifically named here for the first time in this gospel. (The term occurs a hundred times in the New Testament.) The word evidently means "separated ones." This sect arose during the times of the Maccabees with the good purpose of withstanding the rising tide of worldliness among the Jews. The Pharisees stood for strict observance of the Mosaic law with all its ceremonial requirements. By the time of Christ they had become legalistic, and some of them hypocritical.

When they saw Jesus eating with the tax collectors and sinners, these Pharisees found fault. Perhaps afraid to tackle Him as yet, they complained to His disciples. This is the second conflict the Pharisees had with Jesus. The first was over His claim to forgive sins (2:7).

When Jesus heard the criticism of these teachers of the law, He declared that it was the sick, not the well, who need a physician. He came "not to call the righteous, but sinners" (v. 17). (The added words *to repentance* are not in the oldest Greek manuscripts.) A physician is supposed to come into contact with diseased people in order to help them medically.

How much more should the great Physician associate with those diseased by sin in order to heal them! If the medical doctor will risk physical contagion, why should He shrink from the danger of ceremonial contamination? If we are His followers, we must follow Him in this ministry to those in need spiritually.

11. **The Dispute About Fasting (2:18-22).** This is the third conflict between Jesus and the teachings of Pharisees. It happened on a particular day that the disciples of John and of the Pharisees *were fasting*—not "used to fast" (v. 18). This time the critics (cf. Mt 9:14) came directly to Jesus. They asked Him, "Why are the disciples of John and the disciples of the Pharisees fasting, but your disciples are not fasting?" This more precise translation of the Greek points up the concrete situation that precipitated the conflict. It was a fast day for the Pharisees. The disciples of John the Baptist joined them in observing it. But the disciples of Jesus—evidently following His example—were not fasting.

Only one fast day was prescribed by the Old Testament law. That was the annual Day of Atonement (Lev 23:27). On that day the people were to confess their sins. The high priest was to slay a goat as a sin offering and sprinkle its blood on the mercy seat over the ark in the holy of holies, thus making an atonement for the sins of the people.

But the Jews had added many fast days to their calendar. They fasted on the anniversary of the destruction of Jerusalem by the Babylonians in 586 B.C. and in memory of other calamities in their history. By the time of Christ the Pharisees also made a regular habit of fasting twice a week (Lk 18:12), on Mondays and Thursdays.

The Master defended His disciples in their freedom. Could the children of the bridechamber (v. 19)—the members of the bridal party or the close friends of the bridegroom—fast while the bridegroom was with them? The obvious answer is no. People do not fast during a wedding!

But Jesus went on to say that the time would come when the bridegroom would be taken away, and then His friends would fast. The meaning seems clear. When the heavenly Bridegroom would be taken away from His disciples, they would fast and mourn His absence.

In verses 21 and 22 we find two short parabolic statements rising out of Jesus' discussion with the Pharisees. In the first He declared that no one would sew a patch of nonpreshrunk cloth on an old garment. If he did, when the garment was washed the patch would shrink and tear away at the edges. Thus a worse rent would be made. The spiritual religion, Christianity, was not to be patched on to legalistic Judaism.

The second figure is equally graphic. No one puts new wine into old *wineskins*. (They did not have bottles in those days.) If he does, the new wine will ferment, expand and burst the old wineskins. That happens because they had already stretched when filled previously with other fermenting wine. Now there was no more stretch in them. So the leather would give way, and both the wine and the wineskins would be lost. New wine must be put into new wineskins. The fresh leather will then expand as the fermentation takes place, and all will be well.

The application is obvious. If the new, fresh wine of Spirit-filled Christianity were to be poured into the old dry, rigid wineskins of legalistic Judaism, both Christianity and Judaism would perish. The Christian movement could not remain a sect of Judaism and survive. The freedom of the Spirit would burst the restraining bonds of legalistic Pharisaism, but there was danger that both would perish in the process. Jesus was clearly indicating that His gospel must find expression in a new movement.

These two brief parables were given by Jesus in answer to

a question about fasting. He refused to lend His endorsement to the legalistic type of fasting prescribed by the Pharisees as a religious duty. If it is to have a spiritual value, it must be spontaneous and voluntary. When one fasts in order that he may give himself to earnest, uninterrupted praying, the fasting will have real benefit. If it induces pharisaic pride, it does more harm than good.

12. **Working on the Sabbath (2:23-28).** This occasioned the fourth conflict between the Pharisees and Jesus. It so happened that on a Sabbath day He and His disciples were walking through *grainfields*. The translation "cornfields" (v. 23) reflects British usage and misleads an American reader. What is called "corn" in the United States was unknown in the Old World. In fact, wheat is still referred to as "corn" in the British Isles.

As they walked along the narrow path through the field of grain the disciples began to pluck the *heads of grain*—not "ears of corn." Probably the grain was wheat, though it may possibly have been barley. The latter was eaten by the poorer classes.

The Pharisees observed what the disciples were doing and immediately complained to Jesus. Why were His followers doing on the Sabbath "that which is not lawful" (v. 24)?

It should be pointed out at once that there was no suggestion that the disciples were stealing. The Mosaic law specifically stated that a person could help himself to the heads of wheat when walking through someone's fields of grain, though he was not to cut any with a sickle (Deu 23:25). The objection the Pharisees made was that the disciples were working on the Sabbath. Plucking the grain was reaping. Rubbing off the husks was threshing. And blowing the chaff out of their hands was winnowing! This is a good example of how picayunish legalism can become.

Jesus answered their criticism by calling attention to what David did (v. 25). Fleeing from Saul, he became hungry. At the house of God the high priest informed him that only shewbread (v. 26), or "bread of the Presence," was available. This was sacred and was supposed to be eaten only by the priests. Yet David and his followers ate it. The satisfying of human need is more vital than the observance of religious ritualism.

Here Jesus was meeting the Pharisees on their own ground, for the rabbis had faced up to the problem inherent in this scripture (1 Sa 21:1-6). Their conclusion had been that David was justified in eating the sacred bread rather than starving. They rightly asserted that God's laws were given that men might live, not die.

The words "in the days of Abiathar the high priest" (v. 26) have caused much discussion. In 1 Samuel 21 it is stated that Ahimelech, Abiathar's father, was the priest at the tabernacle when David came and asked for food. The best interpretation is to take the phrase above as meaning "in the lifetime of Abiathar the high priest." It would then be similar to saying that a certain event happened "in the days of George Washington, the first President of the United States." This would not necessarily indicate that the event took place while Washington was in office. Perhaps here Abiathar's name is used because he became the prominent high priest in David's reign.

The Jewish rabbis had a saying: "The Sabbath is delivered unto you, and ye are not delivered to the Sabbath." Jesus put it even more explicitly: "The sabbath was made for man, and not man for the sabbath" (v. 27). Good laws do not exist for their own sake, but for the benefit of mankind. Especially was this true of the commandment to remember the Sabbath day and keep it holy. Man needs one day a week away from his work. He needs it for rest of his body and mind, and spiritual refreshment for his soul. Adam Clarke comments, "Had we no Sabbath, we should soon have no religion."

The last verse (28) goes a step further: "Therefore the Son of man is Lord also of the sabbath." Someone has well said that Jesus is Lord of the Sabbath "to own it, to interpret it, to preside over it and to ennoble it, by merging it into the Lord's day."

How should we observe the Lord's Day? The simplest answer is By doing those things, and only those things, that we believe would be pleasing to the Lord of the Sabbath. There is room here for considerable freedom of the Spirit in interpreting precise rules and regulations. But if we submit fully to the lordship of Jesus and seek to please Him every day—not simply on Sunday—we shall live satisfying and effective lives.

13. The Man with the Withered Hand (3:1-6). This is the fifth conflict of the Pharisees with Jesus. Back at Capernaum again (cf. 1:21; 2:1), He went into the synagogue. In the service that morning was a man whose hand was withered—literally, "having been dried up." The Pharisees present watched him (v. 2), to see whether He would heal the man on the Sabbath day, "that they might accuse him." The Greek says, "They kept watching Him closely." Wycliffe, in his English version of the Bible, caught the idea correctly. He translated it: "Thei aspieden Hym." The Pharisees were acting as spies, trying to trap Jesus. There is a bare possibility that they had "planted" the afflicted man there to see what Jesus would do about it. In other words, they hoped He would heal the man so that they could get Him into trouble. This is religion "gone sour."

The Jews permitted healing on the Sabbath only if there was danger the person might die before the next day. Obviously this man's case was not that kind of an emergency; he could wait a few hours longer. In the eyes of the Pharisees healing was working. A person could take medicine to ease pain; but a poultice could not be applied on the Sabbath day, for drawing the pus to a head would be working! All these minute details are spelled out in chapter after chapter of Sabbath day regulations in the Jewish rabbinical writings.

Doubtless Christ was conscious of the attitude of His critics who were sitting there watching Him narrowly. He could have waited until after the service and arranged a secret healing of the man at Peter's house that afternoon. Instead He made the thing as public as possible. If the Pharisees wanted to know what He would do, He would give them full opportunity to find out. So He called to the man, "Stand forth" (v. 3)— literally, "Rise into the midst." Everyone was to have a chance to see what happened.

As the whole crowd sat there tensely waiting to see the next act in the drama, Jesus turned to the Pharisees and asked whether it was "lawful to do good on the sabbath days or to do evil? to save life, or to kill?" (v. 4). His enemies had hoped to trap Him. Now He trapped them with a question which obviously had only one answer. But they were not willing to give that. They "held their peace"—or, "kept silent." It was the stubborn, sullen silence of those who dare not publicly give the wrong answer but refuse to come through with the right one, lest they incriminate themselves.

There are two possible applications of Christ's double question. The first is that if a man does not do good when he can, he thereby does evil. James Morrison comments, "To refuse to do good is to choose to do evil."

The second part of the question suggests the other application. The word translated "save" is used in the gospels, Acts, and the epistle of James for physical healing. But it also occurs throughout the New Testament with the meaning of spiritual salvation. While Jesus was planning to heal the man on the

Sabbath, the pious Pharisees were plotting to kill Him (v. 6). Who was really desecrating the Sabbath day?

What is proper for us to do on the Lord's Day? Christ's answer is clear. Whatever is good and helpful to humanity is lawful. Whatever harms or hurts is wrong. If we make Sunday a solemn, dismal day in our homes, we are damaging our children, not saving them. We may turn them permanently against the church and against God Himself. Sunday should be the brightest, happiest day of the week.

Should a Christian ever be angry? Christ was! But we need to note carefully what is said here. "Looked around" (v. 5) is in the aorist tense, suggesting a momentary flash of anger. On the other hand, "being grieved" is in the present tense of continuous action. It indicates a constant state of grief over the sins of the people. Jesus was angry at the callous, cruel attitude of the Pharisees toward human suffering and need. The Christian who has the keen moral sensitivity of his Master will also at times feel a Christlike anger against human wrong. We cannot truly love God unless we hate sin.

Jesus was "grieved for the hardness [better, hardening] of their hearts." The term suggests moral insensibility or callousness. The Greek word used here is the equivalent of the Latin *callus*. Both terms were used in the medical language of that day for a hardening substance on a broken bone. Some Pharisees had become so rigid in their legalism that it made them callous and careless in the face of human suffering. It is a false religion which affects one that way.

Having set the stage with the afflicted man standing out in the middle where everybody could see him, Jesus now gave the order, "Stretch forth thine hand." How could he? The man might have argued, "I can't!" Instead he willed to move his hand. As he did so, Christ supplied the power. Faith is the attitude of obedience. God answers with ability. Our whole responsibility is to obey. It is God's obligation to furnish the enablement. As soon as the man asserted his will to stretch out his withered hand, it extended normally from his body like the other.

Instead of rejoicing that the man was healed, the Pharisees stalked out of the synagogue and held counsel (v. 6) with the Herodians as to how they might destroy Jesus. They had not profited at all by Christ's question about saving or killing on the Sabbath.

The Herodians are named only three times in the New Testament (cf. Mk 12:13; Mt 22:16). While Josephus, the Jewish historian of the first century, does not mention them, it is obvious that they were supporters of Herod Antipas, ruler of Galilee and Perea. That is, they were in favor of Roman rule. The Pharisees, on the other hand, hated this foreign domination. They were strong nationalists. Ordinarily they would have nothing to do with the Herodians. But they linked up with them in a common opposition to Jesus. This league against Him soon made it necessary for Him to leave Galilee.

14. The Popularity of Jesus (3:7-12). In spite of the opposition of the religious and political leaders, Jesus enjoyed a season of great popularity with the common people. But He had to leave the city. He "withdrew himself with his disciples to the sea" (v. 7). There on the shores of the Lake of Galilee a great multitude gathered round Him.

The division between verses 7 and 8 should be placed after *followed him*. The new sentence (and verse) would then be "And from Judaea . . . a great multitude [v. 8] . . . came unto him." That is, the people of Galilee, where He was, followed Him; but also people from distant parts came to Him.

Judaea was far to the south, with its capital, Jerusalem, a hundred miles from Capernaum. Yet people walked all this distance to come to Jesus. They even came from Idumaea,

which was south of Judea. This is the only place in the New
Testament where Idumea is named; it is a modification of
"Edom."

People even came from "beyond Jordan"; that is, Perea,
which means "across." In Jesus' day it, along with Galilee, was
ruled by Herod Antipas. More surprising, pilgrims came from
the northern area "about Tyre and Sidon." These were two
main cities of ancient Phoenicia, the country now called
Lebanon. Hearing about the miracles of Jesus, they came to
see Him.

So great was the crowd that Jesus had to get into "a small
ship" (v. 9). "Boat" would be more accurate. This probably
was Peter's fishing boat, which was anchored near shore. Here
the multitude of people could see and hear Him. He was
afraid the crowd would throng (crush) Him.

The reason was that "he had healed many" (v. 10). So the
people "pressed upon him"—literally, "they were falling on
Him." All the sick were trying to touch Him, until He was in
danger of being pushed bodily into the lake.

Again we find demons confessing the deity of Jesus (v. 11),
and once more He muzzles them (v. 12). The demonic revelation of His Messiahship could cause more harm than good.

15. The Appointment of the Twelve (3:13-19). Jesus went up
into a nearby mountain (v. 13), or "hill," and called to Himself
a special group of disciples. The power of His personality is
shown by the fact that "they came unto him."

Of these He "ordained twelve" (v. 14)—better, "appointed"
them. The Greek simply says "made." Their call was twofold:
first to "be with him," and second "that he might send them
forth to preach." This underscores the fact that a call to preach
presupposes a call to prepare. And the most important preparation is being with Jesus and learning from Him. Along with
this must come formal education and learning all we can from

others. These apostles were also "to heal sicknesses, and to cast out devils [demons]" (v. 15).

Verses 16-19 contain the names of the twelve apostles whom Jesus chose. Similar lists appear in Matthew 10:1-4; Luke 6:13-16; Acts 1:13. In every case Peter's name heads the list and that of Judas Iscariot comes last—except in Acts, after his death. All the lists divide naturally into three groups with four names in each (with the exception of the group in Acts). The first group is always composed of the four fishermen.

Simon (v. 16) was the most common Jewish name in the first century. Jesus gave His follower the new name *Peter* (Greek *petros,* stone). This is the first of nineteen times that the name *Peter* occurs in this gospel, which reflects his vigorous personality and preaching.

James and *John* were nicknamed *Boanerges* in Aramaic, meaning "Sons of thunder" (v. 17). The reason for this is not readily apparent. We know that they wanted to call down fire on a Samaritan village (Lk 9:54). James was the first apostolic martyr (Ac 12:2), perhaps because of his thunderous witness. The writings of John, especially the book of Revelation, have heavy tones of thunder.

Thaddaeus (v. 18) is evidently the same one who is called "Judas the brother [or, son] of James" in Luke 6:16; Acts 1:13. Perhaps because of the defection of Judas Iscariot, this Judas preferred to be known as Thaddaeus. *Simon the Canaanite* should be "Simon the Cananaean." Luke identifies him as "Simon called Zelotes"; that is, "the Zealot." We do not know whether this means he was zealous for Christ or whether he had belonged to the rising nationalistic party of Zealots, who later revolted against Rome (A.D. 66-70).

Judas Iscariot, as usual, is identified as the one "which also betrayed him" (v. 19). *Iscariot* is usually considered to be the Greek equivalent of the Hebrew *Ish-Kerioth* (man of Kerioth).

There was a town named Kerioth in southern Judah (Jos 15:25). If this identification is correct, Judas Iscariot was the only one of the twelve apostles who came from outside Galilee. This may have caused him finally to feel an antipathy toward Jesus and His Galilean disciples.

16. Opposition from Friends and Foes (3:20-27). It is obvious that the last clause of verse 19, "and they went into an house," belongs with verse 20. A more accurate translation is "And He comes home," that is, to Peter's house in Capernaum.

Again the crowds gathered. So busy were Jesus and His disciples "that they could not so much as eat bread" (v. 20). This was the period of popularity for Christ.

But now came opposition—which usually follows popularity. News of His strenuous life got back to His "friends" (v. 21). The literal translation is "those from beside Him." In the papyri of that period it meant "family," and that is probably the best rendering here. Jesus' relatives in Nazareth *went out* to stop Him from His mad career. They said, "He is beside himself"—literally, "He is standing out of himself"; that is, "He has gone out of his mind."

Some scribes "came down from Jerusalem" (v. 22). The Jews always spoke of going "up" to Jerusalem and "down" from it when they left their sacred capital. Jerusalem is situated on an elevation of approximately 2,500 feet above sea level, but these words were used also to express honor and are still used today for that purpose. These scribes had walked one hundred miles northward from Jerusalem to check on this upstart prophet from Nazareth. They had their explanation for Jesus' "crazy" zeal: "He hath Beelzebub." (This comes from the Latin; the Greek manuscripts have Beelzebul or Beezebul.) It was by the prince or ruler of the demons that He was casting out the demons. It is significant that they did not question the fact that He did cast them out.

Christ summoned His critics and challenged their accusations. He showed that their position was wholly illogical. "How can Satan cast out Satan?" (v. 23). A kingdom (v. 24) or a house (v. 25) "divided against itself . . . cannot stand." Likewise if Satan should rise up against himself he would come to an end (v. 26). No one can plunder a man's house without first binding the strong man (v. 27). By this last statement Jesus intimated that He had already conquered Satan and was now robbing him of his demonic power on earth.

17. The Unpardonable Sin (3:28-30). Now Jesus sounds a serious warning against the attitude of the scribes. All sins and blasphemies (v. 28) will be forgiven to men except the blasphemy "against the Holy Ghost" (v. 29). The one who commits this sin will never have forgiveness. He is "in danger of eternal damnation." The best Greek text says, "is guilty of an eternal sin," or "is held in the grip of an eternal sin." This is the worst fate that could come to any individual—instead of salvation, no escape from sin forever. This is the most horrible hell that one could imagine.

What is "the unpardonable sin"? What does it mean to "blaspheme against the Holy Ghost"? Verse 30 suggests that the scribes had committed this sin or at least were in danger of doing so. What they had done was to attribute the work of the Holy Spirit to Satan. Jesus had been anointed by God with the Holy Spirit and performed His miracles by that power. The scribes had witnessed God's power but had called it Satan's power. Augustine defined this sin as a willful persistence in impenitence and unbelief. It is deliberate moral confusion, calling light darkness and darkness light.

Some people have been obsessed with the fear that they have committed the unpardonable sin. They should find comfort in these words of the devout Bishop J. C. Ryle: "There is such a thing as a sin which is never forgiven. But those who are troubled about it are most unlikely to have committed it."

18. The True Family of God (3:31-35). About this time Jesus' brothers and mother appeared. It may well be that they had started out from Nazareth that morning (v. 21), walked the nearly twenty-five miles to Capernaum, and now arrived (v. 31) as evening came on. The dispute with the scribes (vv. 22-30) took place between their departure and arrival.

It might be assumed that Jesus' family came to comfort Him. But verse 21 suggests another purpose. They were going "to lay hold on him" and take Him home. Standing outside, they sent a message in to Him, asking Him to come out (v. 31).

When this was reported to Jesus (v. 32), He "looked round about on them which sat about him" (v. 34). The Greek adds "in a circle." This is another example of Mark's attention to the looks and gestures of Jesus. Probably sweeping the crowd with His hand, the Master said, "Behold my mother and my brethren!" Then He stated quite categorically that His family consisted of those who "do the will of God" (v. 35). It was not that Jesus did not love His earthly family. But He was enunciating the principle that the highest relationships of life are spiritual, not physical.

19. The Parable of the Sower (4:1-20). This is one of the longest of Jesus' parables, and it is found in all three synoptic gospels (cf. Mt 13; Lk 8). It was appropriately delivered in the open air on the shores of the Lake of Galilee. Again (cf. 3:9) the crowds were so great that Christ "entered into a ship, and sat in the sea" (v. 1)—that is, of course, in the ship on the lake. The thousands of people sat on the sloping bank of the shore. It formed a natural open-air theater to carry His voice up the hill.

The Master's usual method with large crowds was to speak in parables (v. 2)—from the Greek *parabolē* (something placed beside, a comparison). These were stories that illustrated a truth vividly. *Doctrine* should be translated "teaching."

To the crowd on shore Jesus cried, "Listen! Look!" (v. 3). Perhaps at that very moment there was a man striding across a nearby field in plain sight scattering wheat seed with broad sweeps of his hand. This can still be seen in Palestine.

As the man was sowing, some seed fell "by the way side" (v. 4), or "along the path." Some fell "on stony ground" (v. 5)—in thin soil on top of a ledge of solid rock. The warm, moist soil in such a natural "hot bed" would cause the seed to spring up quickly, without much root. But the sun would soon dry out the thin layer of soil. The plants would be scorched and wither away (v. 6). Other seed "fell among thorns" (v. 7). Growing faster than the wheat, the weeds would choke out the plants and prevent their reaching maturity. But some seed "fell on good ground" (v. 8) and yielded a good crop.

For obvious reasons this interesting story is often called the parable of the *soils*. The point of the parable turns on the difference between the four kinds of soil, rather than on the person of the sower. To underscore the importance of this parable Jesus added, "He that hath ears to hear, let him hear" (v. 9). According to the synoptic gospels the Master sounded this solemn warning on five occasions. The words also occur eight times in the book of Revelation.

In verses 10-12 Jesus gives His reasons for speaking in parables. At the close of the day He was alone with His followers, who sought an explanation of His parables (v. 10). (*Parable* is plural in the best Greek texts.) He told them that they had the privilege of understanding "the mystery of the kingdom of God" (v. 11). While the word *mystery* (Greek *mustērion*) occurs in the gospels only in connection with this parable, Paul uses it twenty-one times in his epistles. In the New Testament *mystery* refers to something known only by divine revelation. Others expected the kingdom of God to come with outward pomp and glory. The disciples were to understand that it is a spiritual kingdom or reign of God in the hearts of those who believe in Jesus Christ. For outsiders truth must come in parables.

Verse 12 is one of the most difficult passages to interpret in this entire gospel. It is based on Isaiah 6:9-10. If we interpret "that" as meaning "so that" (result) rather than "in order that" (purpose), the matter becomes clearer. It should be noted that purpose and result are two sides of the same coin and that sometimes the same expression can be interpreted either way. Also it has been suggested that Jesus used parables so that hard hearts would not reject plain truth. Perhaps later His hearers would remember the stories and understand and accept their meanings.

In verses 13-20 we have the Master's own explanation of the parable of the sower. The seed is the Word (v. 14). The soil of the wayside (v. 15) typifies "hardened hearts," that do not even receive the truth. The stony ground (v. 16) symbolizes "shallow hearts," that respond to the truth with emotional enthusiasm but have no depth of moral and spiritual character. Such people "have no root in themselves" (v. 17) and so are easily offended or fall away. Those among thorns (v. 18) are the ones who accept the message; but the truth is choked out of their "strangled hearts" by three types of thorns (v. 19): (1) "the cares of this world," or anxieties of the age; (2) "the deceitfulness of riches," what has well been called the pitiful passion for accumulation; and (3) "the lusts of other things entering in," literally, the desires concerning the remaining things. As Halford Luccock has pointed out, *miscellaneous things* can become the greatest cause of spiritual strangulation.

There is a fourth soil, the "good ground" (v. 20) of receptive hearts. But even here there is a gradation—"some thirty-fold, some sixty, and some an hundred." We should pray that we may bring forth fruit—the inward "fruit of the Spirit" (Gal 5:22-23) and the outward fruit of winning souls to Christ—in the largest measure possible.

20. Parabolic Sayings (4:21-25). *Candle* (v. 21) should be translated "lamp," for people did not have candles in the time of Christ. They used little clay lamps filled with olive oil and having a small wick protruding. Many of these from Roman times have been found in archaeological excavations in Palestine. *Bushel*, the Roman *modios*, was more the size of a peck measure and was used as a container for flour. *Bed* is "couch." *Candlestick*, of course, should be "lampstand." This was usually a niche in the wall of the one-room home, which was often without windows. Jesus intimated that a lamp would not be brought into the house to be hidden under the grain measure or couch; rather it is brought to be placed on the lampstand where it can light the home.

Then He made the application. There is nothing hid which will not be manifested, nor kept secret except finally to come abroad (v. 22). As the saying goes, "Things are hid because they are precious, but precious things are meant to be used at sometime and in someway."

Again (cf. v. 9) Jesus sounds the admonition: "If any man have ears to hear, let him hear" (v. 23). We are responsible to listen carefully and then obey.

The second parabolic saying here is found in verses 24-25. The Master first warns, "Take heed what ye hear." Then He asserts that we shall receive an amount in accordance to the size of the receptacle we use. He adds: "And unto you that hear [carefully listen] shall more be given." The better we listen, the more we gain. The meaning of this verse may be explained in the context as follows: "Your attention to the teaching will be the measure of the profit you will receive from it." The truth of this statement is so obvious as to need no elaboration.

Verse 25 may not seem quite as clear. Yet the principle is just as universally valid. Those who have spiritual truth will receive more. But the one who has failed to listen and profit by what he hears will soon be deprived of what little he possesses. The old adage fits here: "Use or lose."

21. The Parable of the Seed Growing Secretly (4:26-29). This is the only parable found in Mark's gospel alone. It probably occurs here because of its relation to the parable of the sower. Even with good seed sown in good soil, growth and production take time. Patience is needed. After a man has "cast seed into the ground" (v. 26) he will "sleep and rise" (v. 27) many times before the harvest comes. The earth brings forth fruit by itself (v. 28). The Greek is *automatē* (automatically), found only here and in Acts 12:10 ("of his own accord"). First the blade appears, then the ear (head), then the full corn in the ear (full grain in the head). When the grain has matured, the harvest is reaped with a sickle (v. 29).

This parable has an important message for all who sow the Word of God. When the seed has been faithfully sown, it should be given time to grow. We should not expect a full crop of Christian graces immediately. Nevertheless, we may water the seed with our tears and prayers (cf. Ps 126:5-6).

22. The Parable of the Mustard Seed (4:30-32). This parable also relates to the sowing of seed. It is found in all three synoptic gospels. It is one of the many parables of the kingdom.

Jesus said that the kingdom of God is like a grain of mustard seed (v. 31). When planted in the ground it is "less than all the seeds that be in the earth." This statement has been challenged. Actually, the mustard seed is not the smallest seed known to botanists. But it evidently was the smallest in common use among the Jews. It was proverbial for something small (cf. Mt 17:20).[1] Palestinian mustard is about the size of our petunia seed.

Yet, when this tiny seed is planted in the ground, it becomes "greater than all herbs, and shooteth out great branches" (v. 32). The Talmud speaks of climbing up on a mustard tree as one would on a fig tree. Large mustard trees may be seen in various places in Palestine. One outside the Church of Mary and Martha in Bethany stands to a height of well over twelve feet.

The traditional interpretation of this parable applies it to the growth of the Christian church during this age. Though it had a very small beginning in Palestine, it has spread throughout the world. The Jewish rabbis referred to Gentile nations as "the birds of the air." People of all nations today are found resting in the shelter of the true church of Jesus Christ. Some modern writers give an opposite interpretation: The rapid growth of the mustard tree symbolizes the development of a great world church, with wicked "birds" in its branches. The traditional view seems to fit better into the context of Jesus' teaching here.

23. Many Parables (4:33-34). Mark reports that "with many such parables" Jesus spoke the Word to the people, "as they were able to hear it." To the multitudes He spoke only in parables and then explained these privately to His disciples.

24. The Stilling of the Storm (4:35-41). This miracle is recorded in all three synoptic gospels. Mark gives us Peter's eyewitness account, told in vivid fashion.

For many weeks Jesus had been teaching the large crowds that thronged around Him on the heavily populated west shore of the Lake of Galilee. He was weary, almost worn out. So He suggested to His disciples that they "pass over unto the

[1]See W. Harold Mare, "The Smallest Mustard Seed—Matthew 13:32," *Grace Journal,* IX (Fall, 1968), pp. 3-11.

other side" (v. 35). The eastern shore was relatively uninhabited. There they could find relaxation and rest for both body and mind.

Having dismissed the crowds, they "took him even as he was in the ship" (v. 36)—probably Peter's fishing boat again. "Other little ships" went along. The seasoned fishermen were used to making the voyage of six or eight miles across the lake.

So tired was the Master that He went to the stern of the boat, stretched out on the cushion on the steersman's seat, and was soon fast asleep (v. 38). The measure of His weariness is shown by the fact that the "great storm of wind" (v. 37) which came up did not waken Him. Starting with a sudden flapping of the sails, the wind soon whipped up high waves that broke over the bow of the boat. The King James Version says that finally the boat was *full*. Of course, if this had been true the boat would have been at the bottom of the lake. The Greek clearly says the boat "was already filling." They could not bail out the water fast enough.

Alarmed at the violent squall and the rapidly filling boat, the disciples wakened Jesus, crying out, "Master, carest thou not that we perish?" Standing to His feet, He looked into the teeth of the howling gale and uttered just two words. The first was *Peace* (v. 39), or "Be silent!" The second word literally means "Be muzzled and stay muzzled!" Creation heard the voice of its Creator. Immediately the wind ceased to rage and the waves to roll, "and there was a great calm." Anyone acquainted with the water knows that waves continue to dash high for some time after a heavy wind stops blowing. This was a double miracle.

To the disciples Jesus said, "Why are ye so fearful?" (v. 40). Seasoned sailors though they were, they had shown cowardly terror. The Master that day taught His disciples that the cure for fear is faith.

Now they "feared exceedingly" (v. 41) in a different way. This time it was awe in the face of the majestic power and presence of Christ. Fear of God eliminates cowardly fears.

25. The Gerasene Demoniac (5:1-20). Jesus and His disciples continued to the other (eastern) side of the Lake of Galilee, into the country of the Gadarenes (v. 1). This incident is recorded in all three synoptic gospels. The King James Version has *Gadarenes* in Mark and Luke, *Gergesenes* in Matthew; but the best Greek text has *Gerasenes* in Mark and Luke, *Gadarenes* in Matthew. All of these names were apparently given to the territory east of the Lake of Galilee. The area may have been under the influence of Gerasa (modern Jerash), one of the cities of the Decapolis (5:20).

The Master and His disciples had gone to the eastern shore to seek solitude and rest (cf. 4:35). On the way over they had passed through a terrible storm. Now another storm awaited Him—a tempest inside a demon-possessed maniac.

As soon as they stepped on shore, the silence was shattered by bloodcurdling shrieks. Looking up the hillside the disciples saw a beastlike man, naked, disheveled, dirty, rushing down toward them. The disciples would have turned to the boat and pushed off from the shore for safety. But then they saw that their Master was standing fast. They waited to see what would happen.

A threefold description of the demoniac is given in verses 3-5. First, he "had his dwelling among the tombs." He was actually living in the midst of death. In the second place, "no man could bind him," not even with chains. When this had been attempted, he had torn apart the chains around his wrists and broken in pieces the fetters around his ankles. So fierce was he that no man could tame him. In the third place, he spent his nights in the hills and tombs, "crying [out] and cutting himself with stones." Here we have a threefold picture of sin. We see that sin is suicide, insanity and self-destruction.

When the man spied Jesus, he ran and worshiped Him, that is, "fell at his feet" (v. 6). He cried out, addressing Christ as "Jesus, Son of the most high God" (v. 7). He begged the Master not to torment him. James says in his epistle, "The demons also believe, and tremble" (Ja 2:19).

As Jesus had rebuked the storm on the lake, so He now rebuked the unclean spirit (v. 8) in the poor demoniac. Pressing the case further, He "asked him [probably the demon], What is thy name?" The answer was "My name is Legion: for we are many" (v. 9). This shows the utterly confused state of the man inside; he was all mixed up—*my, we*. The same thing shows up in the next verse: "He besought him much that he would not send them away out of the country" (v. 10). Who is *he? Them?*

Nearby was a large herd of hogs feeding on the hillside. The demons begged to be allowed to go into the swine (v. 12). It is notable that they knew they were subject to Christ's command. When He gave His permission, the unclean spirits (v. 13) went out of the man and entered the hogs. The result was disastrous. The whole herd of two thousand stampeded down the mountain side into the lake and were drowned.

The swineherds fled and reported in the city and in the country what had happened (v. 14). The people came to Jesus, perhaps intending to punish Him for destroying their hogs. But when they saw the former uncontrollable demoniac "sitting, and clothed, and in his right mind . . . they were afraid" (v. 15)—that is, filled with awe at this display of divine power. Those who had witnessed the miracle told these newcomers what had happened to the demoniac, but "also concerning the swine" (v. 16). The result was that they (v. 17)—perhaps the owners of the hogs—begged Jesus "to depart out of their coasts [borders]." If Christ was going to interfere with their business, they did not want Him around. They preferred to have their hogs than to have the compassionate Healer in their midst. Today the world is making the same choice in most cases. That is why affairs are in such a sad state. If one wonders why Jesus allowed such destruction of property, it is helpful to remember that pigs were classed among the unclean animals in the Mosaic law code (Lev 11:7; Deu 14:8).

When Jesus went aboard the boat, the healed demoniac asked for the privilege of going with Him (v. 18). But Christ bade him go back home and tell his friends "how great things" (v. 19) the Lord had done for him. Eagerly the man carried out the orders of his new Master. He published abroad in the Decapolis what Jesus had done for him. *Decapolis* means "ten cities." The name was given to a league or federation of cities, all of which were east of the Jordan Valley, except for Scythopolis, which was on the west side of the river. These cities stretched from Damascus in the north to Philadelphia (modern Amman) in the south.

Hitherto Christ had been commanding those He healed not to say anything about it. Why did He change this time? The answer is probably to be found in the fact that He was now in a foreign area where popularity would not hinder His work or threaten His safety. The cured man's preaching actually prepared the way for Jesus' later ministry in the Decapolis (7:31).

26. The Raising of Jairus' Daughter (5:21-43). This section actually includes two miracles; but the healing of the woman with the hemorrhage is sandwiched in the middle of the story about Jairus' daughter, so that it is difficult to treat the two incidents separately.

When Jesus returned to the west side of the Lake of Galilee a large crowd quickly assembled. This was the constant pattern at this stage of His ministry. As usual, the throngs gathered on the shores of the lake, so that Christ was "nigh unto the sea" (v. 21).

Out of this vast crowd one man pressed his way through to Jesus. Jairus was "one of the rulers of the synagogue" (v. 22). In this position of authority it would be his duty to have charge of the services there, choosing the ones who would say the prayers and read the Scripture selections. Thus he would be a leading person in his community, held in high honor.

In spite of his dignified office, Jairus fell at the feet of Jesus and besought Him to come and heal his daughter. With parental anguish he said, "My little daughter lieth at the point of death" (v. 23)—literally, "is at her last gasp." But he had faith that if the Master would come, his little girl would be healed and live. Probably Jairus had been present in the synagogue at Capernaum when Jesus healed the man with the withered hand (3:1-6). He also would have heard about the many miracles Christ had performed. All he wanted now was the healing touch of the Master's hand.

Jesus did not need any urging. He was always ready to meet human need and answer the call for help. So He went with Jairus. As usual, "much people followed him, and thronged him" (v. 24)—literally, "pressed Him together." That is, they were pressing Him on all sides. For this reason progress would be rather slow.

As the company moved on toward the home of the synagogue ruler, an interruption took place. In the crowd was a woman who had had a hemorrhage for twelve years (v. 25). By now her case had been given up as hopeless. With a typical disillusioned layman's point of view Mark records that she "had suffered many things of many physicians," that she "had spent all that she had, and was nothing bettered [benefited], but rather grew worse" (v. 26). Luke, "the beloved physician"

(Col 4:14), when recording the same incident in his gospel, is careful to protect his profession. He says that the woman "could not be healed of any" (Lk 8:43). That is, hers was an incurable illness.

But Mark, probably here reflecting Peter's report again, was fully justified in what he says about the physicians taking all the woman's money without doing her any good. The Jewish rabbis had a saying, "The best physician is worthy of Gehenna [hell]." Adam Clarke quotes from the rabbinical writings five Jewish prescriptions for a woman with an issue of blood. One of them runs like this: "Set her in a place where two ways meet, and let her hold a cup of wine in her hand; and let somebody come behind and affright her, and say, Arise from thy flux." The others consisted of weird concoctions given her to drink.

Doubtless the woman had long since given up all hope of finding any help. But news about Jesus' miraculous healings had kindled a new glimmer in the darkness. "Perhaps He can heal me too." When she heard that the great Physician had arrived back on the western shore, she joined the people thronging to Him. Coming up in the press (crowd) behind Him, she "touched his garment" (v. 27). Her faith was that if she could even touch His robe she would be *whole* (v. 28)—literally, "saved." Immediately "the fountain of her blood was dried up" (v. 29). She "felt [knew] in her body" that she had been healed from her plague (scourge). The tingling sensation of new health went through her being.

But someone else was conscious that something had happened. Jesus knew "that virtue [Gr., *dynamis*, "power"] had gone out of him" (v. 30). It cost Jesus personally to perform these miracles! He turned around in the crowd and asked, "Who touched my clothes?" His disciples expostulated, "You see the crowd pressing around you, and yet you say, 'Who touched me?'" (v. 31, RSV). Many people were pressing against Jesus on every side, but only one touched Him by faith. How similar is the situation today! Of the millions who attend church services every Sunday morning, how many touch Christ by faith for spiritual blessing?

Paying no attention to the impatient remark of His disciples, Jesus kept on looking around "to see her that had done this thing" (v. 32). The woman began to tremble with fear. According to the Mosaic law (Lev 15:25-27) she was unclean, and she defiled all those whom she touched. So technically she had rendered Jesus unclean. But here is the glory of grace. Instead of the woman contaminating Christ by her touch, "power" had gone out of Him and cured her.

Finally the woman fell down before Jesus and "told him all the truth" (v. 33). Why did He insist on her making a public confession? Because He wanted to give her an added benediction. This is the only recorded place where Jesus addressed a woman as *daughter* (v. 34). How comforting that term must have sounded to her! He assured her, "Thy faith hath made thee whole"—literally, "has saved you." Then he added, *"Go in peace and be whole* [*hygiēs*, "healthy"] *of thy plague."* It would seem that the great Physician healed her soul as well as her body. While it is true that the verb *save* (Gr., *sōzō*) is used for both physical healing and spiritual salvation, peace comes only through the forgiveness of sins.

All this time Jairus was standing there, doubtless becoming more anxious and disturbed with every passing moment. Why did Jesus waste a lot of time talking to a woman when his daughter was dying at home? It was a trying time for the synagogue ruler, who was accustomed to getting first attention from others.

While Jesus was still talking, a messenger came from Jairus' house with sad news: "Thy daughter is dead: why troublest thou the Master any further?" (v. 35). One does not have to use his imagination much to interpret the probable attitude of the messenger. Doubtless it showed in the tone of his voice. "The teacher doesn't care about your daughter. If he did he would have hurried to the house. Here he is, talking with this woman! Don't bother with him anymore."

Jesus "heard the word that was spoken" (v. 36). But *heard* is more accurately translated "ignored." The same Greek word is rendered "neglect to hear" in Matthew 18:17. In the Septuagint (Greek version of the Old Testament) this word regularly has the meaning "hear without heeding," or "take no heed." Jesus paid no attention to the rather obvious implication of the messenger's words. Instead He turned to Jairus and said (literally), "Stop being afraid; just keep on believing." Under the circumstances it was a tremendous challenge to the synagogue ruler's faith.

The Master took with Him only three of His disciples: Peter, James, and John (v. 37). These same men were later alone with Him on the mount of transfiguration and in the garden of Gethsemane. They composed the inner circle of Christ's followers.

When they arrived at Jairus' house (v. 38), they found everything in a "tumult" (uproar). Hired professional mourners wept and wailed—the louder the better! With neighbors and relatives adding to the din, the noise must have been almost unbearable.

Entering the home, Jesus chided them, "Why make ye this ado?" (v. 39)—or, "Why are you making an uproar?" Then He shocked them by asserting, "The damsel is not dead, but sleepeth." By this He meant that her death was only temporary. But the mourners took Him literally and turned into mockers: "They laughed him to scorn" (v. 40). This was no atmosphere of faith for performing a miracle. So Jesus "put

them all out." Then He took the girl's parents and His three
disciples and went into the room where the dead body lay.

Taking the girl by the hand, He said, "Talitha cumi" (v. 41).
This is Aramaic for "Damsel, arise." It has been suggested
that these may have been the very words with which the little
girl was wakened by her mother each morning. Here we see
the human tenderness of Christ, as well as His divine power.
What a beautiful combination!

Immediately the girl arose and walked (v. 42). Now her
age is given—twelve years. Probably it is only a coincidence
that the woman just healed by Christ had suffered her hemorrhage for *twelve years.*

Again Jesus commanded silence about the miracle. He was
seeking to avoid any crowds with political ideas about His
Messiahship. He instructed the parents to give the girl something to eat (v. 43). Here we find the important principle that
Christ does for us what we cannot do for ourselves, but what
we can do is our responsibility.

These two intertwined miracles might be taken as symboliz-
ing two types of sinners. First are those who come to Jesus
with their sense of need, as the woman did. The second are
helpless, as was Jairus' daughter. They need to be helped by
friends or loved ones if they are to find Jesus.

27. The Rejection at Nazareth (6:1-6). Jesus went out from
Capernaum and "came into his own country" (v. 1), or childhood home, Nazareth. This was a day's walk of about twenty
miles.

When the Sabbath came, "he began to teach in the synagogue" (v. 2). He was back in the "home church" that He had
attended as a child and young man. His former friends and
neighbors were *astonished* at His teaching. Where did He get
His wisdom? He had never been to a rabbinical school. After
all, He was simply their village carpenter (v. 3). He was the

son of Mary, which implies that Joseph was dead. Four of His brothers are named. *James* later became head pastor of the Jewish Christian church at Jerusalem (Ac 12:17; 21:18). He acted as moderator of the Jerusalem Council (Ac 15:13-21), and is thought to be the author of the epistle of James. *Jude* is held to be the author of the epistle of Jude. Nothing is known about the other two brothers or the sisters who still lived in Nazareth. Knowing Jesus' humble background, His fellow townsmen "were offended at him."

In reply to their attitude Christ repeated a familiar proverb: "A prophet is not without honour" (v. 4) except at home. Today we say, "Familiarity breeds contempt."

Because of the unbelief of the people of Nazareth, Christ "could there do no mighty work" (v. 5). He healed a few sick folk, but that was all. He "marvelled" (v. 6) at their unbelief. Only on one other occasion is Jesus said to have marveled. That was when He witnessed the great faith of a foreigner (Mt 8:10). (This strange contrast still appears sometimes today.) Unable to help His former acquaintances at Nazareth —their unbelief robbed them of His ministry of mercy—Christ "went round about the villages, teaching." In other places His presence was welcomed.

28. The Mission of the Twelve (6:7-13). It was some time since Jesus had appointed His twelve apostles (3:13-19). Now that they had been with Him for a period of training, they were ready to go out and preach (cf. 3:14).

The wise Master sent out His disciples "by two and two" (v. 7), as Mark alone notes. This procedure has been followed from time immemorial. The advantages are obvious. One can help the other in times of danger, discouragement, doubt or illness. As He dispatched them, pair by pair, He gave them "power [authority] over unclean spirits." Mark especially emphasizes the work of Jesus and His apostles in casting out demons.

He also gave them careful instructions for their journey. They were not to carry any unnecessary luggage. Each one was allowed to take along one "staff" (v. 8), or walking stick. Matthew 10:10 and Luke 9:3 seem to prohibit even this. But probably the meaning is that if anyone did not have a staff he was not to acquire one. They were not to take a "scrip"—a bag for carrying food—nor bread, nor money. That is, they were allowed no food, no wallet for carrying food that might be given, and no money for buying food. (In the best Greek text *bread* comes before *scrip*.) They were to trust God and depend on the hospitality of the people. It must be remembered that Palestine has a warm climate, it was the custom to entertain passersby for meals and lodging, and their missionary tour was to be of short duration. Alfred Plummer puts the matter well: "Make no elaborate preparations, as if you were going a long journey on your own business; you are going a short journey on mine." They were to wear sandals (v. 9), and not carry an extra pair of shoes (Mt 10:10). Nor were they to have two coats. The Greek word indicates the tunic, or undergarment worn at that time. This was to be a brief, intensive tour, and the missionaries must travel light.

Another important admonition was given. The apostles were to abide in one place while they were in any community (v. 10). This would avoid the ever present danger of carrying gossip from house to house, as well as the danger of offending one family by seeking a better home.

If the people of any place refused to receive them or listen to them, they should leave. As they departed they were to "shake off the dust" (v. 11) from their feet as a testimony against the town. Paul and Barnabas did this at Pisidian Antioch (Ac 13:51). It was a symbolic act, signifying that the city was reckoned to be heathen, rejected by God because it had rejected His messengers. (The last sentence of verse 11, referring to Sodom and Gomorrah, is not in the best Greek manuscripts.)

The apostles "went out, and preached that men should repent" (v. 12). This was the same message that both John the Baptist and Jesus Himself had proclaimed. They also cast out many demons and "anointed with oil" (v. 13) those who were sick, healing them. Another place where anointing with olive oil is mentioned in the New Testament is in James 5:14. The Orientals believed that this oil had medicinal value (cf. Ps 23:5; Lk 10:34). Anointing with oil symbolized the fact that God was pouring out His grace on the afflicted. It seems to have been used as an aid to faith.

29. The Death of John the Baptist (6:14-29). The miracle-working ministry of Jesus was reported to King Herod (v. 14). Herod Antipas was ruler of Galilee and Perea (4 B.C.–A.D. 39). He was actually only a tetrarch, as Matthew and Luke correctly call him, who inherited part of the kingdom of his father, Herod the Great. But in Rome it was the custom to refer to all native rulers in the East as kings, and Mark was writing for the Romans. It is also possible that Herod Antipas was popularly called "King Herod" in Galilee.

When Herod heard about what Jesus was doing, his conscience rose up to plague him. He thought that John the Baptist, whom he had beheaded some time before, had risen from the dead. No one else could be carrying on in this way. Others thought it was "Elias" (v. 15)—that is, Elijah. (It is best always to use the Old Testament form for Old Testament names when they occur in the New Testament.) Still others said it was a prophet. But Herod declared, "It is John, whom I beheaded" (v. 16). His guilty conscience confronted him afresh.

The story of John the Baptist's death is a sordid tale. Herod

Antipas had gone to Rome, where he stayed in the home of his half brother Philip. He repaid his host's hospitality by stealing his wife, Herodias. She deserted Philip. Herod divorced his own wife, the daughter of Aretas, king of the Nabatean Arabs, and brought his new wife back to Palestine.

It is no wonder that the righteous soul of John the Baptist was stirred to indignation. Very undiplomatically, but as a faithful prophet of God, he said to Herod, "It is not lawful for thee to have thy brother's wife" (v. 18). The predictable result was that "Herodias had a quarrel against him [literally, "had it in for him"] and would have killed him; but she could not" (v. 19). Why not? "For Herod feared John . . . and observed him" (v. 20). The Greek says, "kept him safe." Apparently Herod kept John locked up in prison so that Herodias could not have the annoying prophet assassinated. Meanwhile Herod listened to John and "did many things." Two of the best Greek manuscripts say, "was much perplexed." Herod and Herodias form a striking parallel to Ahab and Jezebel in the Old Testament. In both cases the husband was weak and vacillating, the wife wicked and scheming.

Just as Jezebel plotted the death of innocent Naboth, so Herodias conspired to kill John the Baptist. But she bided her time. Finally the "convenient" (opportune) day came (v. 21). Herod was planning a great birthday feast in his own honor. All the notables of his realm were to be there—the "lords [civil magistrates], high captains [military commanders], and chief estates [leading men] of Galilee." When the men were intoxicated, or nearly so, and their moral inhibitions were loosened, Herodias sprang her trap. She was so desperate in her hatred of John the Baptist and in her desire to kill him that she was willing to degrade her own daughter, Salome, as Josephus the historian named her. No real princess would think of dancing like a slave girl. But Herodias would balk at nothing. She sent her young daughter into the banquet hall to put on a sensuous dance in front of the drinking guests. The plot worked. Salome pleased Herod (v. 22) and his guests. The drunken king promised under oath to give the girl whatever she asked, "unto the half of my kingdom" (v. 23). The trap had sprung. Through her daughter, the mother—cool, cruel, crafty—sent in her demand: "The head of John the Baptist" (v. 24). The girl hurried back in and asked for the prophet's head "in a charger" (v. 25)—that is, on a platter. ("By and by" should be "at once.")

Shocked into soberness, the king was exceeding sorry (v. 26). He had been trying to keep John from being killed, but his wife had outwitted him. Unfortunately, there were the guests, who had heard his oath. He could not afford to "lose face" with the group. So he "immediately"—to get the bad business over with—sent an executioner (v. 27), who beheaded John in prison. The head was brought on a platter and given to the damsel (v. 28), who gave it to her mother. Human hate was satiated with the sacrifice.

The disciples of John the Baptist heard the sad news. They picked up the corpse (v. 29) of their beloved leader and laid it in a tomb.

The sequel to this story is of interest. Herodias later became jealous because a brother of Antipas had received the official title of king. She urged her husband to go to Rome and obtain his honor. Instead, he was sent into exile. The only good thing that can be said for Herodias is that she voluntarily went into exile with him.

30. The Feeding of the Five Thousand (6:30-44). Verse 30 gives the return of the twelve apostles and their report on their mission. They told Jesus "both what they had done, and what they had taught." The word *apostle* (Gr. *apostolos*) means "one who has been sent on an errand." It basically means the same as *missionary,* which comes from the Latin.

The feeding of the five thousand is the only miracle of Jesus recorded in all four gospels. This, of course, does not include the resurrection.

After their strenuous missionary tour the twelve apostles needed a rest and change. The Master would care for His men. So He said to them, "Come ye yourselves apart into a desert place, and rest a while" (v. 31). For again (cf. 3:20) they were so busy with the constant crowds that "they had no leisure so much as to eat." Getting into a boat they departed privately (v. 32) to a desert place—that is, a lonely, uninhabited area, such as could be found on the east side of the lake.

But their vacation plans went awry. For many saw them departing (v. 33) and recognized who He was. Eager to be with Christ, they ran on foot around the north end of the Lake of Galilee while the disciples went across by boat. The slowness of travel on the water is shown by the fact that those who traversed a greater distance on land outwent the disciples and arrived first on the eastern side. When Jesus came out of the boat, He saw a great crowd awaiting Him. Instead of resenting their interruption of His vacation plans, He "was moved ["gripped"] with compassion toward them, because they were as sheep not having a shepherd" (v. 34). He began to teach them. Jesus did not look at a crowd as a mass or mob. He saw people as individuals needing help.

As evening drew on, the disciples became concerned. They had many guests on their hands, and no food. Anxiously they came to Jesus and reminded Him that it was a desert place (v. 35) with no markets nearby. They suggested that He send the people away to buy (v. 36) food at the neighboring farms or villages. But Christ presented them with a startling challenge: "Give ye them to eat" (v. 37). They protested that if they had "two hundred pennyworth of bread" it would not be enough. The penny was the Roman *denarius*, representing a full day's wages.

In reply Jesus asked His disciples how many loaves (v. 38) they had. (The "loaf" was the size of a small, flat bun.) They answered, "Five, and two fishes." The Master of the situation gave instructions to have the crowd "sit down by companies [recline company by company] upon the green grass," thereby confirming the statement in John 6:4 that the feeding of the five thousand took place shortly before the Passover (Mar.-Apr.). The grass in Palestine is green only in the spring.

So the people reclined "in ranks" (v. 40). The Greek has *prasiai prasiai*—flower beds, flower beds. This probably reproduces Peter's reaction as he saw the people in their colorful Oriental garments, grouped by hundreds and fifties on the green grass of the hillside.

With everything arranged in orderly fashion, Jesus was now ready to serve the evening meal. He took the five loaves and two small fish, looked up to heaven (v. 41) in a prayer of blessing, then broke the loaves and gave the food to His disciples to distribute to the people. The same was done with the fish. The result: "they did all eat, and were filled" (v. 42). The last word, in the original, suggests that the hungry people were satisfied; they had all they wanted.

Then the waiters received their "tips" for serving the people. Each of the twelve apostles filled his lunch basket with the fragments (v. 43) left over. The number who had eaten was "about five thousand men" (v. 44).

One obvious lesson comes out of this miracle. Jesus said to the disciples, "You give them to eat." This was impossible, preposterous. Yet the twelve did exactly that; they served the whole crowd of five thousand men. Christ furnished the power to multiply the few loaves and fishes. But His disciples cared for the distribution. When God gives a command, He also gives the ability to carry it out, if we obey.

31. Jesus Walking on the Water (6:45-52). As soon as the crowd had been fed, Jesus immediately "constrained" (v. 45)— a strong word meaning "compelled"—His disciples to embark in the boat and return across the lake. Why this urgency? The answer is found in John's account of the feeding of the five thousand. It was because the people wanted to take Him and make Him king (Jn 6:15). The ambitious disciples would have fallen in with this idea enthusiastically. If Jesus could feed such a crowd with a few morsels of food, He could drive out the Roman rulers and also supply the Jews with all their material needs. But this is precisely what Christ was seeking to avoid. So He must get the disciples at once out of this revolutionary atmosphere.

The apostles were told to go across "to the other side . . . unto Bethsaida." But the only Bethsaida (which means "house of fish") we know about was on the east bank of the Jordan River just north of the Lake of Galilee. Perhaps they tried to cross the narrow bay to this city but were driven back by northerly winds so that they had to go to the western side. Or perhaps a fishing village near Capernaum was also called Bethsaida.

When Jesus had dismissed the crowd, "He departed into a mountain to pray" (v. 46). By now Peter's boat was "in the midst of the sea" (v. 47). As dusk came on, Jesus could see His disciples "toiling [distressed] in rowing" (v. 48) because they were facing into a strong wind. About the fourth watch of the night (3:00-6:00 A.M.) He came to them, walking on the water. It looked as if He were going to pass them by. The disciples thought He was a ghost, and they cried out (v. 49) with fear. But immediately (v. 50) He comforted them by identifying Himself. His words still come with assurance to us in the dark hours of life: "It is I; be not afraid."

As soon as Jesus got into the boat with His fearful disciples, the wind ceased (v. 51). The men were "sore [exceedingly] amazed." They had forgotten the miracle of the loaves which they had just witnessed, "for their heart was hardened" (v. 52). Their lack of faith had made them spiritually dull.

32. Ministry in the Plain of Gennesaret (6:53-56). The plain of Gennesaret was on the west shore of the Lake of Galilee, not far south of Capernaum. As soon as Jesus disembarked, immediately the people knew Him (v. 54). At once they began hurrying around, bringing sick people on beds—quilts used as stretchers—to the great Healer "where they heard he was" (v. 55). Wherever Jesus went, into villages, or cities, or country (v. 56)—this takes in all kinds of dwellings—they laid out the sick, asking that they might touch at least "the border of his garment." This is perhaps better translated "the tassel of His robe," the blue-banded fringe which the Law required all male Jews to have on the corners of their outer garments (Num 15:38). This distinguished the Jews from the Gentiles. Jesus observed the Law and so dressed in this way.

The plain of Gennesaret was one of the most fertile areas in all Palestine. It was here that Jesus enjoyed great popularity and ministered to multitudes of people.

33. Conflict with Pharisees over Cleansing (7:1-23). In chapters 2 and 3 we found Christ in conflict with the Pharisees over Sabbath observance. Now there comes a clash with them over the other most important question in their eyes, that of ceremonial defilement.

Again (cf. 3:22) there were scribes from Jerusalem (v. 1), more than a hundred miles away, who were collaborating with local Pharisees in opposing Jesus. Watching for an opportunity to criticize, they observed some of His disciples eating with *defiled* hands (v. 2). The adjective literally means "common," which with the Jews had the technical sense "ceremonially unclean." Mark explains that this meant "unwashen." This does not imply that the disciples were eating their food without washing their hands at all, but they had failed to wash in the prescribed ceremonial fashion.

For the benefit of his Roman readers, who would be unfamiliar with Jewish customs, Mark adds the explanation (v. 3) that the Pharisees in particular and Jews in general did not eat without first washing their hands "oft"—literally, "with the fist." The exact meaning of the term here is unknown. Some think it means "up to the elbow." Taken literally it would suggest washing one hand with the closed fingers of the other. Perhaps the best translation is "diligently." The picture seems to be similar to that of doctors or nurses scrubbing their hands before an operation.

In this meticulous ceremonial washing the Pharisees were following "the tradition of the elders." (The phrase occurs only here in vv. 3 and 5, and in the parallel passage, Mt 15:2.) This expression refers to a body of minute regulations which had been handed down orally from the leading rabbis of the past. These were later put in written form. The rabbis sought to protect the sacred law of Moses by putting a "fence" around it in the form of detailed rules which would regulate every aspect of daily conduct. But this made religion a grievous burden which Peter later said "neither our fathers nor we were able to bear" (Ac 15:10).

Continuing his explanation, Mark says that when the Jews came from the market (v. 4), where they might have been contaminated by the jostling throngs, they would not eat until they first wash—literally, "sprinkle themselves." These strict Pharisees not only washed their bodies but also gave careful attention to the ceremonial washing—literally, "baptisms"—of

cups, pots (pitchers), and brasen (brass or copper) vessels
(cooking utensils). (The oldest Gr. manuscripts omit *tables*—
lit. "couches.") The Jewish Mishna devotes no less than thirty
chapters to the cleansing of vessels.

The Pharisees and scribes (v. 5) now ask Jesus why His
disciples do not walk (live) "according to the tradition of the
elders, but eat . . . with unwashen [common] hands." In reply
Christ cited a prophecy from Isaiah. The quotation in verses
6 and 7 is taken from Isaiah 29:13, which well described the
hypocritical attitude of substituting the tradition of men for
the commandment of God (v. 8). Incidentally, the word
hypocrites (v. 6) is found in Mark only in this verse. (It is
used 13 times in Mt and 3 times in Lk.) It was used for actors
on the stage, who wore large masks containing small mega-
phones to amplify their voices. So a hypocrite is a playactor
who plays his role insincerely, appearing to be what he actually
is not.

Then Jesus applied these words of Isaiah to His present
critics. "Full well ye reject the commandment of God, that ye
may keep your own tradition" (v. 9). He proceeded to give an
illustration. "Moses said, Honour thy father and thy mother"
(v. 10). This was one of the Ten Commandments (Ex 20:12).
The one who cursed his parents should die (Ex 21:17). But
the tradition of the elders had circumvented this. It permitted a man to say to his needy parents, *Corban* (v. 11). This
is a Hebrew word which Mark explains for his Gentile readers
as meaning a "gift," or something vowed to the Lord. There is
evidence from Jewish writings of this cruel custom of permit-
ting a man to say to his parents, "I have devoted to God that
which otherwise I would use for your support." He was then
legally free from his obligation to care for his father or mother
(v. 12). Ambrose of the fourth century made this apt comment: "God does not seek a gift wrung out of the necessities

of parents." Christ concluded with the charge that the Pharisees were "making the word of God of none effect through your tradition" (v. 13). They had come to Him criticizing His disciples for failure to wash their hands ceremonially before eating, in obedience to the tradition of the elders. He turned on them the far more serious accusation of using that very tradition to set aside the clear commands of God's Word. For good measure He added, *"and many such things ye do."*

Then Jesus summoned the crowd again (v. 14) and explained the source of real defilement. Nothing entering (v. 15) a man can defile him, but only those things which come out of him. A person is not defiled by the food he eats but by the thoughts which emerge from his wicked heart. Jesus thus pointed out the basic difference between His religion and that of the Pharisees. They gave primary attention to the outward, formal observance of prescribed rules and regulations. His emphasis was on the inner attitude and motive. When any religion places more value on the outward than the inward, it has ceased to be true religion; it is decaying. This danger faces every religious movement.

Finally Jesus left the crowd and went back into Peter's house. There "his disciples asked him concerning the parable" (v. 17). The reference is evidently to the brief parabolic saying of verse 15. Surprised by their ignorance, Jesus answered, "Are ye so without understanding also?" (v. 18). Certainly the disciples should have comprehended their Master's statement, even if the crowd did not.

Patiently Christ explained that food cannot defile a man because it does not go into his heart (v. 19) but into his stomach and then is taken care of by the digestive processes which eliminate what is harmful. The form of the Greek suggests that "purging all meats [food]" is not a part of Jesus' question but should be placed separately as a comment by the writer: "In saying this He made all food clean." That is, Christ's teaching here canceled all distinctions between "clean" and "unclean" foods, on which the Jews put major emphasis. Peter had to receive a special vision on the housetop at Joppa (Ac 10:15) before he could grasp the full implication of what His Master said here. Peter evidently emphasized this truth in his preaching thereafter, and Mark has given us here the inspired interpretation of what Jesus meant.

Verses 21-23 are an elaboration of the general statement in verse 20. Christ went on to particularize by specifying the "evil thoughts" (v. 21) that come out of men's hearts. The list of sins given here is similar to what we find in Paul's epistle (e.g., Gal 5:19-21). Mark names twelve: six in the plural and six in the singular. He goes all the way from adulteries and fornications to pride and foolishness (v. 22). The so-called sins of the spirit are just as wicked in God's sight as the sins of the flesh. *Foolishness* refers to the attitude of making sin a joke—"the stupidity of the man who lacks moral judgment." This is one of the greatest evils of modern society.

34. The Syrophoenician Woman (7:24-30). Twice already Christ had withdrawn with His disciples from the crowded west shore of the Lake of Galilee. Both times they went across to the east side of the lake. In the first instance He cured the Gerasene demoniac (4:35—5:20). In the second He fed the five thousand (6:30-44).

On this third withdrawal He rose "from thence [Capernaum]" and went far northward forty or fifty miles to the borders of Tyre and Sidon (v. 24). This was ancient Phoenicia, modern Lebanon. There He entered a house, so as to be alone with His disciples. The obvious purpose of this "retreat" was to instruct His twelve apostles and prepare them for the time when He would leave them to carry on His work.

But He could not be hid. Hearing that the famous miracle-worker from Galilee had come to her area, a woman "whose young daughter had an unclean spirit" (v. 25) sought Him out and fell at His feet in earnest entreaty. By language she was Greek, by race a Syrophoenician (v. 26), a descendant of the Canaanites (cf. Mt 15:22). Phoenicia was the seacoast section of southern Syria. Mark, writing at Rome, uses the term *Syrophoenician* to distinguish her from the Libyo-Phoenicians of North Africa around Carthage.

The woman asked Jesus to cast the devil (demon) out of her daughter. At first sight His reply (v. 27) seems harsh and cruel. He said that the children (Jews) should first be fed, for it was not meet (good) to take the children's bread and throw it to the dogs (Gentiles). It seems out of character for the Master to call a Gentile a "dog," though this was a regular practice of the Jews of that day. But perhaps Christ used the term as a backhanded thrust at the bad attitude of His disciples. According to Matthew's account they begged Jesus to "send her away; for she crieth after us" (Mt 15:23). Perhaps they were not very happy about being in this heathen territory. And then to have this Gentile "dog" crying after them! It was just too much to take.

Perhaps the quick-witted woman sensed that Jesus' words were not intended as an insult to her but as a rebuke to the disciples for their narrow, selfish spirit. With magnificent insight she replied, "Yes, Lord: *yet the dogs* [lit., "little dogs," "puppies"]under the table eat of the children's crumbs" (v. 28). What a marvelous combination of humility and faith, as well as keen intelligence! This woman deserved the best, and Jesus gave it to her. He assured her that the demon had already gone out (v. 29) of her daughter. Sure enough, when she arrived home, she found that the demon was gone and her daughter was resting quietly (v. 30).

35. Healing of a Deaf Mute (7:31-37). Leaving the "coasts"

(v. 31)—same word correctly translated "borders" in verse 24— of Tyre, Jesus *went through* Sidon, as the best Greek text says. This would mean that He continued north before swinging south. Returning to the Lake of Galilee, He went down the east side in "the midst of the coasts [borders] of Decapolis." Apparently He was avoiding Galilee, the territory of Herod Antipas, who had killed John the Baptist and was now seeking His death (Lk 13:31). He also probably wished to avoid further conflicts with the Pharisees in Galilee.

The healing of the deaf mute is recorded only in Mark's gospel. The man was "deaf and had an impediment in his speech" (v. 32). This is all one word in Greek, an adjective meaning "speaking with difficulty." The man was not completely dumb, but he could not communicate clearly.

Jesus took the afflicted man "aside from the multitude" (v. 33), in order to give him the quiet, careful attention he needed. Deaf people are normally confused in a crowd. Then the great Physician put His fingers into the man's ears, spat and touched his tongue. "Looking up to heaven, he sighed" (v. 34), and said *Ephphatha*, an Aramaic word meaning "Be opened." The gestures here described were intended to encourage the man's faith. Christ put His fingers into the man's ears and touched his tongue to show that He intended to heal these two areas. The use of spittle was often connected with healing in those days. We find it again in the case of the blind man (8:23) and also the man born blind (Jn 9:6). Vespasian is said to have healed a man with spittle (Tacitus, *History,* IV, 81).

Immediately the man's "ears were opened," the bond of his tongue was loosened, and he "spake plain [straight]" (v. 35). This shows that he had been able to speak, but not so as to be understood.

Again (cf. 1:44; 5:43) Jesus "charged them that they should tell no man" (v. 36). But, as usual, it did no good. Continually they "published" (lit., "were heralding") the miracle. The people were astonished "beyond measure" (v. 37). This is a single word in Greek, meaning "above exceedingly." The spontaneous testimony, "He hath done all things well," finds an echo in the heart of everyone who has felt the Master's touch on his life. Someone has said that these words constitute "a biography of Jesus in miniature." As followers of Christ we should seek to copy His example.

36. The Feeding of the Four Thousand (8:1-10). Once more Jesus found Himself on the east side of the Lake of Galilee surrounded by a large crowd with "nothing to eat" (v. 1). Summoning His disciples, He said to them, "I have compassion on the multitude" (v. 2). The people had been with Him for three days. If He sent them away fasting to their homes, some might become exhausted on the road, having come a long way.

The disciples wanted to know where they were going to get food there in the wilderness (v. 4) to feed such a vast crowd. This question of the apostles has evoked much comment from some critics. In the light of the feeding of the five thousand, how could Jesus' companions be so stupid as to talk this way again? (Cf. 6:35-36.) But the trouble was that the disciples had not learned the lesson of the former miracle. Furthermore, their question may be interpreted as suggesting: "Whence . . . unless you provide?"

Again the Master asked, "How many loaves have ye?" (v. 5). The answer this time was "Seven." Once more He commanded the crowd to "sit down [recline] on the ground" (v. 6). Taking the seven loaves He gave thanks, broke the biscuitlike bread, and had the disciples serve the people. The same was done with a few small fishes (v. 7) that were available. Everyone had plenty to eat and seven baskets (v. 8) of fragments were left over. This time the crowd numbered four thousand (v. 9). After dismissing the people, Jesus embarked with His disciples and went across to Dalmanutha (v. 10). The location of this place is unknown, but it was evidently on the west side of the lake.

37. The Demand for a Sign (8:11-13). Once more the Pharisees (v. 11) confronted Christ. This time they were *"seeking of him a sign from heaven, tempting him."* The rabbis, according to a later treatise, held that when the Messiah came he would take his stand on the roof of the temple, proclaim the salvation of the people, and show them a light from heaven as a sign of his Messiahship (*Pesikta Rabbati*). This was the sort of a sign the Pharisees demanded.

What was Jesus' reaction? He "sighed deeply" (v. 12)—a single strong word in Greek, found only here in the New Testament. The willful unbelief of the religious leaders disturbed Christ to the depths of His spirit. He declared, "There shall be no sign given unto this generation." How is this to be harmonized with the parallel passages in Matthew 16:4 and Luke 11:29, where Jesus says only one sign will be given, that of the prophet Jonah? In Mark's account it means that no sign of the kind demanded by the Pharisees—a spectacular light from the sky—would be given. Instead they were pointed to the sign already found in God's Word.

Sickened by the unreasonable attitude of His critics, Jesus once more embarked and crossed "to the other side" (v. 13)— presumably the east side of the Lake of Galilee. The Pharisees hounded His trail every time He appeared on the western shore.

38. The Leaven of the Pharisees (8:14-21). The embarkation had apparently taken place rather suddenly—Jesus wanting to get away from the Pharisees—for there were no provisions on board except one loaf (v. 14). The Master took advantage of the opportunity of privacy to warn His disciples to "beware of the leaven of the Pharisees, and of the leaven of Herod"

(v. 15). The former probably referred to hypocrisy, pride and a legalistic spirit. The latter would be worldliness and a desire for political power.

The apostles took Jesus' admonition as a reproof for their lack of food on board. The Master had to chide His disciples for their slowness of understanding and their hardened heart (v. 17), as well as their failure to remember (v. 18). Then He asked them how many basketfuls of fragments they took up after feeding the five thousand (v. 19) and the four thousand (v. 20). Their answers were *twelve* and *seven*. Unfriendly critics have often contended that in the accounts of the feeding of the two great crowds we have two confused traditions of the same incident. But the facts do not bear this out. The feeding of the five thousand is recorded in all four gospels. It is referred to again in Matthew and Mark. In all six references (Mt 14:20; 16:9; Mk 6:43; 8:19; Lk 9:17; Jn 6:13) the same Greek word is used for *baskets*, referring to the small "lunch baskets" of the twelve apostles. The feeding of the four thousand is recorded only by Matthew and Mark and is mentioned again in both gospels. In all four of these references (Mt 15:37; 16:10; Mk 8:8, 20) another Greek word is used, indicating seven larger baskets, or "hampers." This complete consistency should satisfy the demands of any reasonable critic. Even apart from the inspiration of the Holy Spirit it is unbelievable that men who could produce such outstanding books as the gospels by Matthew and Mark would be so careless in handling historical data. A prominent New Testament scholar recently wrote: "Today scholars are no longer inclined to imagine that St. Mark was merely a rather stupid recorder."

39. **The Blind Man of Bethsaida (8:22-26).** The party in the boat finally landed at Bethsaida (v. 22). This was evidently Bethsaida Julias on the east bank of the Jordan River near where it flows into the north end of the Lake of Galilee.

The healing of this person is recorded only by Mark. Jesus "took the blind man by the hand, and led him out of the town" (v. 23), so that He could deal with him privately. Jesus "spit on his eyes, and put his hands upon him." The description here is strikingly similar to the only other miracle which Mark alone records, the healing of the deaf mute (7:33). In both cases we have Peter's graphic recounting of the detailed movements of the Healer.

But this miracle has a unique feature not found in any other incident in the gospels: Jesus healed the man in *two* stages. After the first touch of the Physician's hands on his eyes, the man looked up (v. 24) and reported, "I see men as trees, walking"—literally, "I behold the men, for as trees I see them walking." That is, his partially restored vision enabled him to see what looked like tree trunks. But these were moving; so they must be men. Jesus placed His hands a second time on the man's eyes and "made him look up" (v. 25). This is all one word in Greek. Literally it means, "he saw through," or thoroughly. The mist over his eyes was gone. "He was restored, and saw every man clearly"—rather, "he continued seeing all things at a distance clearly." Now the cure was complete and the man was sent home (v. 26). Again we find the admonition not to tell anyone (cf. 7:36).

Why did this miracle occur in two stages? Alexander Maclaren speaks of Christ "accommodating the pace of His power to the slowness of the man's faith." Certainly the great Physician could have healed this man instantly, as He did in other cases. It seems reasonable to hold that the limitation was on the side of the human, not the divine.

40. Peter's Confession at Caesarea Philippi (8:27-30). From Bethsaida on the northern shore of the lake Jesus and His disciples went about twenty-five miles northward to the vicinity of Caesarea Philippi (v. 27). Herod the Great had built

on the shores of the Mediterranean a splendid city with pro-
tected harbor and called it Caesarea in honor of Augustus
Caesar. His son, Philip, had built a beautiful inland city in
honor of Tiberius Caesar. To distinguish it from the other it
was called Caesarea Philippi. It was situated at the foot of
snowcapped Mount Hermon (elev. 9,232 ft.).

On the way Jesus asked His disciples: "Whom do men say
that I am?" They gave various answers: John the Baptist,
Elijah, one of the prophets (v. 28). Christ preached repentance like John the Baptist, performed miracles like Elijah, and
in general seemed like one of the prophets. Then He asked
them the vital question: "But *you*, whom do you say that I
am?" What others think about Jesus may be interesting, but
what we think is all-important. As spokesman for the group
Peter gave the answer: "Thou art the Christ" (v. 29)—that is,
"the Messiah." The Greek word *christos* and Hebrew word
messiah both mean "anointed one." But though Jesus wanted
His disciples to recognize Him definitely as the Messiah, it was
not time yet to be identified that way publicly. So He strictly
charged His disciples to "tell no man of him" (v. 30).

41. The First Prediction of the Passion (8:31-33). This is the
first of three announcements that Jesus made of His coming
death and resurrection (cf. 9:31; 10:32-34). The expression
"began to teach" (v. 31) highlights the fact that Christ was
making a new departure in His teaching. The confession of
His Messiahship by Peter marks the midpoint of this gospel,
as well as the turning point of Jesus' ministry. A new theme
is introduced: "the Son of man must suffer . . . and be killed
. . . and rise again."

This new teaching could not come until after He had been
accepted as Messiah. On the other hand it was essential that
it be given immediately following the confession, for the disciples shared the erroneous popular conception that the Mes-

siah would come to deliver the Jews from Roman rule. This kind of belief encouraged political revolution rather than spiritual revival. A suffering Messiah was an idea completely foreign to current Jewish thinking. It was altogether necessary for Jesus to warn His disciples that He was going up to Jerusalem not to reign but to die. Yet the events that follow in Mark's gospel show that they failed utterly to understand what He was talking about.

He told them that He would be rejected by "the elders . . . chief priests, and scribes." These three groups comprised the Great Sanhedrin at Jerusalem. *Elders* is perhaps a general name for members of the Sanhedrin. The *chief priests* were Sadducees and had charge of the temple. The *scribes* were mainly Pharisees and taught the Law in the synagogues.

When Jesus began to predict His passion "openly" (v. 32), or "plainly," Peter drew Him aside and "began to rebuke him." But Christ, in turn, "rebuked Peter" (v. 33). Surprisingly He said: "Get thee behind me, Satan [adversary]." These were the same words He had used when the devil tempted Him in the wilderness (Mt 4:10). This does not mean that Jesus was calling Peter the devil. But He saw in Peter's mistaken solicitude the same temptation which Satan had presented to Him at the commencement of His ministry—to avoid suffering and choose the easy way. This temptation was more dangerous as His death drew near. He could not tolerate it for a moment. This is the reason for the strong language here. He warned Peter: "You do not have in mind the things of God but the things of men." Peter was thinking of earthly affairs rather than heavenly truths. He was materially minded rather than spiritually minded. He stumbled over the idea of the cross.

42. The Cost of Discipleship (8:34—9:1). Peter had shown clearly that the way of suffering was abhorrent to him. But the disciple must follow his Master to the cross, in spirit if not in body. So Jesus summoned the people with His disciples and made what is perhaps the most important pronouncement of His ministry: "Whosoever will come after me, let him deny himself, and take up his cross, and follow me" (v. 34). *Deny* and *take up* are both in the aorist tense, suggesting definite decisions of self-denial and crucifixion with Christ (cf. Gal 2:20). But *follow me* is in the present tense of continuous action. Following Jesus is a lifelong assignment, lasting until death.

Verse 35 simply underscores the truth of verse 34. The one who wishes to save his life will ultimately lose it. But the one who loses his life in loving service to others for Christ's sake will find that not only has he saved it but he has multiplied it in those he has helped. It is a simple fact of life that those who try to get all finally lose all, while those who give all actually get all in the end.

Verse 36 has been called "the Parable of the Rich Fool in a nutshell." The rhetorical question is most striking. The only possible answer to it is, "Nothing!" *Exchange* (v. 37) means a price given in exchange for something purchased. If a man has forfeited his soul, the whole world could not buy it back. (The same Gr. word *psychē* is translated *life* in v. 35 and *soul* in vv. 36 and 37.)

Jesus declared that whoever would be ashamed (v. 38) of Him in this wicked generation would discover the Son of man ashamed of him at His return in glory. If we deny Him now, He will deny us then. That points up the connection of this verse with what precedes.

The first verse of chapter 9 belongs at the end of chapter 8. That is the way the division is made in the parallel account in Matthew 16:28. As it stands here in Mark it looks like an introduction to the transfiguration (9:2-8). But to say that *some* who stood there would not "taste of death" before an event that took place a week later seems unreasonable. The whole group of apostles was still alive then.

What, then, did Jesus mean when He said that some who stood there would not die until they saw "the kingdom of God come with power"? The best explanation refers this to the coming of the Spirit at Pentecost and the rapid spread of the church following that epochal event. The language here fits strikingly with what we read about in the book of Acts. The word *power* is *dynamis* (dynamite), the same as in Acts 1:8.

43. The Transfiguration (9:2-8). "After six days"—that is, a week later (cf. Lk 9:28)—Jesus took along with Him "Peter, and James, and John" (v. 2). These are the same three who were with Him when He raised Jairus' daughter. They went up into a "high mountain." This has traditionally been identified as Mount Tabor, in the Plain of Esdraelon a few miles southeast of Nazareth. But that is a rather low mountain (1,843 ft.). Furthermore, its top was the site of a Roman fortress during this period. It does not seem to have been an appropriate place for this event. A more likely location is on one of the southern spurs of Mount Hermon, not far from ancient Caesarea Philippi. There Jesus was transfigured before His disciples. His garments became "shining" (v. 3), or glistening, dazzlingly white.

Moses and Elijah, representing the law and the prophets of the Old Testament, appeared and "were talking with Jesus" (v. 4). Peter was so overwhelmed by this select company that he wanted to make three tabernacles (booths of branches): "one for thee, and one for Moses, and one for Elias" (v. 5).

Poor impulsive Peter, "he wist [knew] not what to say" (v. 6); so he said something! He did not realize the implications of his offer: he was going to put Jesus, Moses and Elijah on the same level, as Islam does. But a "cloud [the Shekinah of God's presence] . . . overshadowed them" (v. 7). A voice from the cloud said, "This is my beloved Son: hear him." This was a rebuke to Peter for speaking out of turn. It was also a rebuke to his idea of putting Jesus alongside Moses and Elijah. Christ alone was the Father's *beloved Son.* They were to listen to Him. At the same time the divine voice confirmed Peter's confession made a few days before at Caesarea Philippi.

Suddenly the cloud and heavenly visitors disappeared. The three disciples "saw no man any more, save Jesus only" (v. 8). This is the test of any vision. If it is a true vision, it will leave us with a renewed sense of Christ's presence.

44. The Question About Elijah (9:9-13). As they were coming down from the mountain, Jesus commanded His three disciples that they should describe to no one what they had seen, "till the Son of man were risen from the dead" (v. 9). After that the story of the transfiguration would become meaningful, because the resurrection would be proof that Jesus was truly the Son of God.

The three men "*kept* [lit., held fast] that saying with themselves" (v. 10). What does this mean? It has been translated "they kept the matter to themselves" (RSV); that is, they did not tell anyone about the scene on the mount. But "held fast" seems to suggest something more. Perhaps the best meaning is "carefully remembered." But what saying did they hold in memory? Probably the reference to His resurrection.

The disciples had a question for their Master, precipitated by the sight of Elijah on the mount. Why did the scribes say that Elijah "must first come" (v. 11)—that is, before the Messiah came? (Mal 4:5). Peter had just confessed the Messiahship of Jesus, and this had been confirmed on the mount by the voice from heaven. But why had not Elijah appeared before Jesus? The answer was that Elijah had come (v. 13)—in the person of John the Baptist (Mt 17:13)—"and they have done unto him whatsoever they listed [wished]." Herod had put him to death.

Verse 12 is more difficult to interpret. How could it be said that Elijah "restoreth all things"? The answer probably is that, as the forerunner, John the Baptist introduced the new order which would eventually bring in the restoration. Perhaps the rest of verse 12 should be translated: "And how has it been written about the Son of man? That He should suffer many things and be despised." Jesus is saying that Old Testament prophecy spoke truly when it predicted the coming of the fore-runner, but it also spoke truly when it foretold the sufferings of the Messiah. That is the connection between the two parts of verse 12.

45. The Epileptic Boy (9:14-29). When Jesus reached the nine disciples left at the foot of the mountain, He saw a great crowd gathered around them, "and the scribes questioning [disputing] with them" (v. 14). As soon as He came near, the people "were greatly amazed, and running to him saluted him" (v. 15). What was the cause of this? The parallel of Moses coming down from Mount Sinai (Ex 34:29) suggests that it may have been the afterglow of the transfiguration that caused such awe and amazement.

At once Jesus asked what the dispute was about (v. 16). One of the crowd answered that he had brought to the disciples his son, who had "a dumb spirit" (v. 17) that tormented the boy unmercifully. Literally he said, "Wherever it seizes him, it dashes him down; and he foams at the mouth and grinds his teeth and becomes rigid" (v. 18). This language indicates that the boy was an epileptic. Matthew 17:15 (RSV) states specifically that he was. The father added: "and I spake to thy disciples that they should cast him out; and they could not."

How disappointed Jesus must have been over this failure of His disciples. He exclaimed, "O faithless generation, how long shall I be with you? . . . bring him unto me" (v. 19). The demon put up one last vicious fight. He "tare" (v. 20)—better, "completely convulsed"—his victim. The boy "fell on the ground, and wallowed foaming." He was a vivid picture of the sinner, lying helpless and hopeless.

Jesus asked the father how long it had been "since this came unto him" (v. 21). The answer was "Of a child"—that is, "from childhood." Often the cruel demon had "cast him into the fire, and into the waters, to destroy him" (v. 22). With anguish in his voice the father pleaded, "But if thou canst do any thing, have compassion on us, and help us." Jesus' reply was literally: " 'If you can!' All things can to him who is believing" (v. 23). In other words, Christ took the *if thou canst* of the distressed father and turned it back to him. What He meant is clear: "The working of this miracle depends on your faith, not on My power alone. There is no question about the latter. But can you believe?" Humbly but earnestly he cried out, "Lord, I believe; help thou mine unbelief" (v. 24).

When Jesus saw a crowd running together, He rebuked the "foul [unclean] spirit": "Thou dumb and deaf spirit, I charge thee, come out of him, and enter no more into him" (v. 25). These last words of command must have brought great comfort to the father. His son would never again suffer from demon possession. But the malicious spirit took out his spite on the boy as he left. With one last shriek he "rent him sore [that is, convulsed him much] and came out" (v. 26), leaving the boy apparently dead. Nothing daunted, "Jesus took him by the hand, and lifted him up" (v. 27). The boy arose.

When they reached the house where they were staying, the disciples asked the question that was bothering them: "Why could not we cast him out?" (v. 28). The Master's answer was "This kind can come forth by nothing, but by prayer" (v. 29).

(The added words, *and fasting,* are omitted in the oldest manuscripts.)

46. The Second Prediction of the Passion (9:30-32). Coming back from the far north, Jesus and His disciples passed through Galilee (v. 30). He was already headed for Jerusalem. His public ministry in Galilee was ended. From now on He would give Himself mainly to the private instruction of His apostles who must soon take His place. So, "he would not that any should know" of His presence in Galilee. Had they known, the multitudes would have flocked to Him once more.

That this was the reason for His secret journey is shown clearly by the words that follow: "For he taught [lit., was teaching] his disciples" (v. 31). What was the central message for them? The Son of man is delivered—"is being delivered," the prophetic present tense of what is sure to take place—"into the hands of men, and they shall kill him; and after that he is killed, he shall rise the third day." The most important truth for the disciples to learn now was their Master's coming death and resurrection. But their spiritual ears were dull of hearing: "they understood not that saying" (v. 32). Probably the hardest thing to understand was the resurrection.

47. Teaching on Humility (9:33-41). For the last time Jesus came to Capernaum (v. 33), which had been the headquarters of His Galilean ministry. *"In the house,"* probably Peter's, He asked a very embarrassing question: "What was it that ye disputed among yourselves by the way?" The disciples held their peace (v. 34). They were ashamed to answer, for on the road they had been arguing as to who would be the greatest. While Jesus was thinking and talking about His coming passion, His followers were filled with pride and selfish ambition. They all wanted the chief place in the Messianic kingdom they expected Him to set up when they arrived in Jerusalem. His mind was set on the cross; they were thinking only about crowns.

So Jesus sat down, as Jewish rabbis always did when teaching, and called the twelve (v. 35). His opening words cut right across their false values of life: "If any man desire to be first, the same shall be last of all, and servant of all." The two marks of true greatness are humility and service. This is one of the most frequently quoted sayings of Jesus in the gospels. Then He illustrated His point by taking a child "in his arms" (v. 36), a typical detail added by Mark. Christian service requires that we *receive* (v. 37)—welcome and treat with kindness—even the least little child.

Jesus had just used the phrase *in my name* (v. 37). Now John reports that they had seen a man casting out demons "in thy name" (v. 38), and they "forbad him" [better, tried to restrain him] "because he followeth not us." Jesus rebuked this narrow spirit of sectarianism. "Stop trying to restrain him," He said (v. 39). "For he that is not against us is on our part" (v. 40). Some scholars have claimed that this is a contradiction of Jesus' words, "he that is not with me is against me," in Matthew 12:30 and Luke 11:23. But the former has to do with outward conduct, while the latter refers to inner attitude. The former relates to our judgment of others, the latter to our judgment of ourselves. One who does the least act of kindness —giving "a cup of water . . . in my name" (v. 41)—will not lose his reward.

48. A Warning Against Giving Offence (9:42-50). John and the other disciples had doubtless given offense to the man they tried to restrain. Now Jesus sounds a solemn warning: "Whosoever shall offend one of these little ones that believe in me, it is better for him that a millstone [lit., a millstone of a donkey, that is, a heavy one rotated by a donkey] were hanged about his neck, and he were cast into the sea" (v. 42). The strong language here underscores the seriousness of this sin

of causing the least humble believer to fall.

There follows the most solemn teaching on hell in the entire New Testament. Jesus said, "If thy hand offend thee, cut it off" (v. 43). The word translated "offend" is *skandalizō*. Perhaps the best rendering here is "cause you to stumble." Jesus said it would be better to cut off your foot (v. 45), or even to pluck out an eye (v. 47), than to be cast into hell. This last word is *Gehenna*. It referred first to the Valley of Hinnom just south of Jerusalem, which was used as the city dump. By Jesus' day the Jews were using the term for the place of future punishment. Christ described it as a place "where their worm dieth not, and the fire is not quenched" (v. 48). (In the oldest Gr. manuscripts vv. 44 and 46, which are repetitions of this, are omitted.) These two figures suggest the gnawing of conscience and the everlasting memory of wrong choice. The metaphors are taken from the city dump with its devouring worms and lurid flames.

Verse 49 is very difficult to interpret. Perhaps the connection with what precedes is that we should be *salted* with the purifying and preserving *fire* of the divine Presence if we would escape the penal fires of Gehenna. Or, the meaning might be that everyone in hell will be salted or preserved with unquenchable fire that preserves like salt instead of destroying.

Jesus now returns to the matter of the argument among His disciples. They were supposed to be the "salt of the earth" (Mt 5:13), but in their selfishness and self-seeking they had lost their *saltness* (v. 50). Jesus admonished them "Have salt in yourselves, and have peace one with another" (cf. Heb 12:14). Salt was used in the East as a sign of the covenant of friendship. The Arabs have a saying, "There is salt between us." That is why *salt* and *peace* occur here together. The salt of God's grace will help us to live in *peace* with each other, instead of quarreling as the disciples were doing (9:33-34).

III

THE PEREAN MINISTRY
10:1-52

1. The Question of Divorce (10:1-12). "And he arose from thence" (v. 1). Thus Mark describes Jesus' final departure from Galilee. Here begins His last, fateful journey to Jerusalem.

He came into the "coasts [borders] of Judaea by the farther side of Jordan." This is what was called Perea, which means "across," that is, across the Jordan River on the east side. Once more great crowds gathered, and "as he was wont"—"as His custom was"—He began to teach. Luke's gospel indicates that He resumed His speaking in parables, which was His regular method with the crowds.

Again the Pharisees (v. 2) appear. This time their question was "Is it lawful for a man to put away his wife?" As was too often the case, their motive was malicious; they were *"tempting him,"* or putting Him to the test. This question of divorce was a dangerous one for Jesus to handle. For He was still in the territory of Herod Antipas, who had divorced his own wife to marry his brother's wife. John the Baptist had been beheaded for criticizing this action. If Jesus condemned divorce, He would risk the same fate. If He condoned it, He would lose the confidence of devout people. Whichever way He answered their question, yes or no, He would be in trouble. As on other occasions, the Pharisees thought they had the Teacher caught in a trap from which there was no escape.

But, as was always the case, they found that they were no match for the Master. The Pharisees considered Moses their highest authority. So Jesus simply parried their question with the logical query: "What did Moses command you?" (v. 3). They replied, "Moses suffered [permitted] to write a bill of divorcement [certificate of divorce], and to put her away" (v. 4). Their answer was based on Deuteronomy 24:1.

But Jesus explained the reason for this concession. It was because of the "hardness of your heart" (v. 5) that Moses wrote this precept. The point was that divorce was already taking place among the Israelites. Moses put limitations on it by requiring a certificate of divorce to be made out, indicating the reasons for the separation. This involved hiring a scribe and going through a legal procedure. Moses was not encouraging divorce but seeking to discourage it.

However, this was not in the original divine plan. "From the beginning of the creation God made them male and female" (v. 6). The last part of the verse is a quotation from Genesis 1:27. The marriage of one man to one woman for life is the foundation of stable society.

Verse 7 and the first clause of verse 8 are a quotation of Genesis 2:24. A man is to *leave* his parents. The Greek has a strong compound verb meaning "leave behind," and so "forsake." Many a marriage founders on the rocks because a husband or wife does not forsake the father or mother. One has to forsake his parents before he can *cleave* to his wife. Again the verb is a strong one: "shall be glued." Modern marriage needs more of the glue of loyal love! (The last clause of v. 7 is missing in some very early manuscripts, but it is unquestionably genuine in Mt 19:5 and Gen 2:24).

Verse 8 expresses a very important truth. Marriage is more

than a business contract. It is a physical and spiritual union which makes it utterly unique. Only as a husband and wife become *one flesh* does the marriage reach its intended consummation. Because of this special union the Pharisees' question can have only one answer: "What therefore God hath joined together, let not man put asunder" (v. 9). *Joined* is literally "yoked." Just as a pair of oxen yoked together—still a familiar sight in Bible lands—had to function in close unity, so should a husband-and-wife team. This is God's plan and it is one of the main secrets of happy living.

When they returned to the *house* (v. 10) the disciples asked for further enlightenment on this subject of divorce. In the safe privacy of the home, where He could speak freely without reprisals from Herod, Jesus stated the matter bluntly: "Whosoever shall put away his wife, and marry another, committeth adultery against her" (v. 11). This is exactly what Herod had done. Then, for his Roman readers, Mark included verse 12. Matthew omits this, because Jewish women did not have the legal right to divorce their husbands. But Greek and Roman wives did.

2. The Blessing of Little Children (10:13-16). This incident follows very naturally the discussion of divorce, for it is usually the children who suffer most in such cases. Children of divorced parents are among the saddest "displaced persons" of our day. Some of them are emotionally damaged for life. They love both father and mother and want to live together with both of them, but the cruel selfishness of the separated parents does not permit it. The anguish and frustration caused in such cases make divorce one of the most serious crimes a person can commit.

Loving mothers brought their children to Jesus in order that He might touch them (v. 13). But the disciples rebuked them. The Master had more important business to take care of than being bothered with children! When Jesus saw this, He was "much displeased" (v. 14)—better, "indignant." He told His disciples to *suffer* (permit) the little children to come to Him, "for of such is the kingdom of God." This could mean either that the kingdom of God belongs to little children or that it is composed of those who have the childlike characteristics of dependence and obedience. Jesus underscored this truth by saying that one who did not receive the kingdom of God as a little child would not enter therein (v. 15). Then with a beautiful gesture of love he took the children "up in his arms [lit., folded them in His arms], put his hands upon them, and blessed them" (v. 16). The Greek word for *blessed* is a strong compound meaning "fervently blessed." Jesus' action was not perfunctory, but fervent. He put His heart into it.

3. The Rich Young Ruler (10:17-22). As Jesus was going out on the road, He was met by an earnest seeker who came running to Him and kneeled (v. 17) before Him. His eagerness is all the more commendable in that he was not asking for material blessing but for spiritual help. His question was "Good Master, what shall I do that I may inherit eternal *life* [that is, the blessings of the Messianic kingdom]?"

The Master's reply (v. 18) seems surprising at first thought. Was He disclaiming deity and sinlessness? So some have said. But this is contrary to the consistent portrait of Jesus in the synoptic gospels. Perhaps what Christ meant was "Why do you call Me good, when you do not accept My deity?" It was a challenge to the seeker to accept Jesus as the Messiah, the Son of God.

Christ then reminded this man of the commandments (v. 19), citing from the Ten Commandments (Ex 20:3-17) five out of the six that have to do with duties toward one's fellowmen. In place of the tenth He substituted "Defraud not." This may have been a special warning to the man, a hint that some of his riches had been gained by defrauding the poor.

The man's answer was "all these have I observed from my youth" (v. 20). He was a fine specimen of manhood. No wonder Jesus "beholding him loved him" (v. 21). But He had to be true to the man's soul. He told him that he lacked one thing —unselfish love for God and man. In order to gain this it would be necessary for him to sell all his possessions, give the proceeds to the poor, "and come, take up the cross, and follow me." Some have considered Christ's instructions here to be a general counsel of perfection: one must take the vow of poverty if he would follow the high road to heaven. But we do not find the Master giving this command to any of His disciples. The obvious fact is that Jesus saw this man had his heart so set on his earthly possessions that he had to part with them entirely before he could have his soul freed from slavery to the material.

The earnest seeker failed the test. Becoming sad (lit., gloomy) he went away grieved (sorrowing), "for he had great possessions" (v. 22). Matthew calls him a "young man" (Mt 19:20). Luke 18:18 identifies him as a "ruler." That is why we refer to him as "the rich young ruler." Presumably he continued to be that. But in choosing the old life of selfishness he rejected the higher way of love which alone can bring joy and peace (Gal 5:22). For a moment there had been a vision of light, but disobedience turned it to darkness.

4. The Danger of Riches (10:23-27). Jesus, too, must have had sorrow in His soul as He watched the young man leaving. Then He turned around toward His disciples and said, "How hardly [with what difficulty] shall they that have riches enter into the kingdom of God" (v. 23). The disciples were astonished (v. 24). The Jews commonly looked on material prosperity as a sign of God's favor. But instead of modifying the statement, Jesus asserted a general truth: "How hard is it . . . to enter into the kingdom of God!" (The words *for them that trust in riches* are not in the oldest Greek manuscripts.) Then He used a graphic hyperbole: "It is easier for a camel to go through the eye of a needle, than for a rich man to enter into the kingdom of God" (v. 25). Efforts have been made to reduce the *camel* to a "rope," or to enlarge *the eye of a needle* to make it represent a "postern gate" through which a camel could only barely squeeze himself. But both ideas are untenable. Jesus painted a perfectly ridiculous picture in order to stamp the truth permanently on the memories of His hearers (cf. Mt 23:24). The Jewish Talmud speaks of an elephant going through a needle's eye. Prosaic-minded Occidentals too often fail to appreciate the poetic imagination of Orientals. It is interesting, too, that Luke uses the word for the "physician's needle" (Lk 18:25), which would further emphasize the idea of an actual needle.

The disciples were still more astonished. If the rich could not enter the kingdom, "Who then can be saved?" (v. 26). Jesus' answer was simple and clear. The impossibility lay only on the human side. "With God all things are possible" (v. 27). Whoever turns fully to God and trusts in Him will find salvation.

5. The Reward of Discipleship (10:28-31). Peter decided that if the rich people could not get into the kingdom, perhaps there was a chance for him to make it! With perhaps some measure of self-righteousness he reminded his Master: "Lo, we have left all, and have followed thee" (v. 28). Overlooking the rather evident selfishness of the remark (cf. Mt 19:27), Jesus assured His disciples that they would not fail to get their reward. Anyone who had left home and family "for my sake, and the gospel's" (v. 29) would "receive an hundred fold" of these in this life, "with persecutions; and in the world to come eternal life" (v. 30). The one who leaves all to go into Christian service finds a hundred houses opened to him with loving hospitality, together with innumerable brethren and sisters in the Lord, mothers in Israel, and children (converts). In a sense all lands are his as he enjoys beautiful scenery he otherwise would not have seen. Along with these come persecutions, which help us on to heaven, where we shall enjoy eternal life. The one who follows Christ all the way simply cannot lose!

One more warning is sounded: "Many that are first shall be last; and the last first" (v. 31). One application of this is that the Jews who were first became last, and the Gentiles who were last became first. The same thing is sometimes true today of those brought up in church and "pagans" from nonchurched homes.

6. The Last Prediction of the Passion (10:32-34). As the group headed for Jerusalem (v. 32), Jesus marched boldly on before, with a determined look on His face. It all seemed very ominous now to the disciples. As they followed Him, they were amazed and afraid. Again He gathered the twelve close to Him and gave the third and final prediction of His passion. As would be expected, He added some details to His previous predictions. In fact, seven phases are enumerated here (vv. 33-34): the betrayal, the sentence of the Sanhedrin, the handing Him over to the Roman authorities, the mockery, the scourging, the crucifixion, the resurrection. Now the picture was complete.

7. The Selfish Ambition of James and John (10:35-45). Right on the heels of this prediction of the passion we find a sad display of self-seeking. The two sons of Zebedee came with a very unreasonable request: "We would that thou shouldest do for us whatsoever we shall desire" (v. 35). In other words, they asked for a carte blanche. When asked what they wanted (v.

36), they requested that they might sit on either side of Him in His glory (v. 37). They had enjoyed the unique privilege of glimpsing this glory on the mount of transfiguration. But they had not profited at all by their Master's teaching about the cross. Jesus told them, in reply, that they did not know what they were asking (v. 38). Were they able to drink of His *cup* (of sorrow) or be baptized with His *baptism* (of suffering)? With pitiful stupidity they replied, "We can" (v. 39). But this ability would come only with the filling of the Spirit at Pentecost. During the harrowing hours of Jesus' suffering they forsook Him. Christ assured them that they would indeed share some of His sorrows. But to give them seats on either side of His throne was not His prerogative. These would be given to those "for whom it is prepared" (v. 40). History demonstrates that important places of service, and often honor, go to those who prepare themselves for such places rather than seek them selfishly.

When the ten (v. 41) heard about the request of their two colleagues they were "much displeased" (indignant). One is tempted to suspect that some of this indignation was prompted by jealousy. In any case, Jesus used the situation as an opportunity for giving His disciples some much-needed teaching on what constitutes true greatness. He called attention to the fact that those who rule the Gentiles "exercise lordship over them [lord it over them] and their great ones exercise authority upon them" (v. 42). But He warned them that it was not to be so in His kingdom. Whoever wanted to be great (v. 43) among them must be their minister (servant), and whoever wished to be the chiefest (v. 44) must be servant (slave) *of all.* As noted before (9:33-37), the marks of true greatness are humility and service. He who excels in these is the greatest in God's sight.

Mark 10:45 is the most significant theological passage in this gospel. Literally it reads: "For even the Son of Man did not come to be served but to serve and to give his life a ransom instead of many." The Greek word for *ransom* comes from a verb meaning "to loose." So the essential idea of ransom is a release. Then it was used, as now, to indicate what was paid to secure that release. In the first century the most common use of the term was for redemption money paid to free a slave. Christ gave Himself as the ransom price to free us from the slavery of sin.

But there is another theological implication here. The preposition translated *for* ("for many") was used in the papyri of that period most frequently with the meaning "instead of." So here it supports the doctrine of Christ's substitutionary atonement, that He died in the sinner's place as a ransom for him. We can rejoice in this gracious truth without indulging in the profitless speculation as to whom the ransom price was paid.

8. The Healing of Blind Bartimaeus (10:46-52). On His last journey from Galilee to Jerusalem Jesus and His disciples passed through Jericho (v. 46). This city was the Jewish city built during Maccabean times down in the Jordan Valley about fifteen miles from Jerusalem. As He was going out of town, accompanied by a sizable crowd, a blind beggar named Bartimaeus sat beside the road. (Luke's account indicates that Jesus was *approaching* Jericho [Lk 18:35], referring to the modern town built by Herod the Great in Graeco-Roman style. Apparently the healing took place halfway between the two towns.)

When Bartimaeus heard that Jesus of Nazareth was passing by, the blind man cried out: "Jesus, son of David, have mercy on me" (v. 47). Apparently he had heard of the healing miracles of Jesus and believed on Him as the Messiah. Many standing nearby told him to hold his peace (v. 48). Instead he yelled more loudly and insistently: "Son of David [a Messianic title] have mercy on me."

Finally Jesus heard the man's cry. He stood still (v. 49) and called for the man to be brought to Him. When the blind man was notified, "he, casting away his garment [his outer cloak] rose, and came to Jesus" (v. 50). The Greek verb tenses underscore the eagerness with which the blind beggar threw off his cloak, leaped to his feet, and hurried to Jesus. When Christ asked what He should do for him, the man made his request brief and definite: "Lord [Rabboni], that I might receive my sight" (v. 51). The Master answered just as briefly (v. 52): "Go, your faith has saved you"—or "made you well." "And immediately he received his sight." From what we have already sensed of the character of Bartimaeus we are not surprised to read that he *followed Jesus in the way*." The imperfect tense suggests that he "kept on following"—presumably up to Jerusalem.

IV

PASSION WEEK
11:1—15:47

1. The Triumphal Entry (11:1-11). Jesus' so-called triumphal entry into Jerusalem on what we now call Palm Sunday was fraught with great prophetic significance. In fulfillment of Zechariah 9:9 He rode into the city on a donkey. By doing so He proclaimed Himself the long-awaited Messiah. It was the public presentation of Himself to the nation. But the religious leaders of the people rejected Him and condemned Him to death. What had started out as a triumphal entry turned out to be a tragedy of tears (Lk 19:41).

Bethany (v. 1) was on the east side of the Mount of Olives, about two miles from Jerusalem (which is west of the mount). The exact location of Bethphage is unknown. As they approached the city, Jesus sent two of His disciples to the village (v. 2) nearby—evidently Bethphage (Mt 21:1)—to get a colt and bring it to Him. If anyone asked why they were untying the colt they were to say that "the Lord hath need of him" (v. 3) and that He would return the colt promptly. Obediently they went, found the colt tied outside in a "place where two ways met" (v. 4)—all one word in Greek, perhaps simply meaning "street"—"and they loose [untied] him."

Some bystanders asked them what they were doing (v. 5), and the disciples replied "as Jesus had commanded" (v. 6).

They brought the colt to Jesus and "cast their garments" (v. 7) on it. Then He mounted the colt. Some zealous followers "spread their garments" (v. 8) on the road as a carpet for Him to ride over. Others spread a litter of leaves on the path. Some ran ahead of Jesus, while others followed. But all were crying out, "Hosanna" (v. 9). Literally this means "Save now," or "Save, we pray." But here it seems to be similar to "God save the King!" The people also cried: "Blessed is he that cometh"—"the Coming One," a Messianic title. Verse 10 also seems clearly to be Messianic. Entering Jerusalem (v. 11), Jesus went into the temple area, looked around, and returned with the twelve to Bethany for the night.

2. The Barren Fig Tree (11:12-14). On Monday morning, as they were coming back into the city from Bethany, Jesus was hungry (v. 12). Some distance ahead He saw a fig tree (v. 13) with leaves on it. So He came, if *haply* (therefore)—because it had leaves—He might find some fruit on it. The fig tree has the unusual characteristic of displaying its fruit before its leaves. Jesus therefore had a right to expect there would be fruit. But when He reached the tree, He found "nothing but leaves." Mark adds: "for the time of figs was not yet." Normally figs are not ripe until June around Jerusalem, and this was only April, when the figs were still green. Because the fig tree was hypocritical, professing what it did not have, Jesus cursed it: "No man eat fruit of thee hereafter for ever" (v. 14).

3. The Cleansing of the Temple (11:15-19). When they again reached Jerusalem (v. 15) Jesus went into the temple area. In the court of the Gentiles, covering several acres, He found a flourishing market, run by the family of the high priest. Here animals approved by the priests were sold to those who needed them for sacrifices. Jesus cast out those who were buying and selling, and overthrew the tables of the money-changers. The requirement was that the temple tax must be

paid annually with the Phoenician silver half-shekel. So the people had to exchange their Greek and Roman money for this. It is claimed that the moneychangers collected about 15 percent for this transaction. It was lucrative but dirty business. Also some people were carrying burdens through the temple court (v. 16), using it as a shortcut from one part of the city to another. Jesus put a stop to this. He said that the temple was to be "the house of prayer" (v. 17), but they had made it "a den of thieves"—rather, "a cave of robbers."

The scribes and chief priests (v. 18) were seeking to destroy Jesus. But because of the popular feeling for Him they did not dare to do anything. Each evening Jesus left the city—probably to avoid the danger of assassination in its narrow streets. He would be safer out at Bethany.

The cleansing of the temple was the second instance of this Messianic act by Jesus. Early in His ministry He had done the same thing (Jn 2:13-22). His action was in line with the prophecy in Malachi 3:1-3.

4. The Lesson of the Withered Fig Tree (11:20-26). On Tuesday morning Jesus and His disciples were returning again to Jerusalem. As they were walking along, they noticed "the fig tree dried up from the roots" (v. 20). Surprised, Peter called Jesus' attention to it; the fig tree He had cursed the day before was already withered away (v. 21).

Using the fig tree as an illustration, Jesus proceeded to give His disciples a lesson on faith. He prefaced it by the general admonition "Have faith in God" (v. 22). Then He made a very challenging statement: One could command a *mountain* (v. 23)—common symbol for a great difficulty—to move into the sea, and if he did "not doubt in his heart, but shall believe that those things which he saith shall come to pass: he shall have whatsoever he saith." This is one of the most sweeping prayer promises in the Bible. Then the Master put it a bit more briefly: "What things soever ye desire, when ye pray, believe that ye receive them, and ye shall have them" (v. 24). Every Christian must discover for himself how he can apply these astounding words to his own prayer life. One thing is obvious: Whatever limitations exist are all on our side. Lack of faith is the greatest hindrance in prayer.

But there is an important condition attached: "When ye stand praying, forgive" (v. 25). We are to forgive others if we expect our heavenly Father to forgive our trespasses. Then the Master issued a solemn warning: "But if ye do not forgive, neither will your Father which is in heaven forgive your trespasses" (v. 26). An unforgiving spirit will form a fatal roadblock in our prayer life. Worse still, if we do not forgive, we shall not be forgiven. We cannot refuse to forgive anyone, no matter what the circumstances, and expect to get into heaven.

5. The Challenge to Jesus' Authority (11:27-33). After the lesson at the cursed fig tree, Jesus and His apostles continued into Jerusalem (v. 27). As He was walking in the temple, He was confronted by the chief priests and the scribes and the elders, who together comprised the Great Sanhedrin. They challenged Him with the question "By what authority doest thou these things?" (v. 28). The reference is obviously to His cleansing of the temple the day before. *What* is literally "what kind of." That is, did He act by divine or human authority?

As on other occasions, Jesus met their question with a counter-question. If they would answer Him, He would answer them (v. 29). His question was "The baptism of John, was it from heaven, or of men?" (v. 30). *Heaven* was a Jewish euphemism for "God." So Jesus was asking them whether John the Baptist's authority was divine or human. The obvious fact is that the same answer fitted both questions. If the religious leaders answered Jesus' question, they would also be answering the question which they had asked Him.

The Sanhedrists "reasoned with themselves" (v. 31). They realized that they were in a tight spot. If—as they really believed—they answered "From heaven," Christ would ask them why they did not believe (obey) John. If they said "*Of men*" (v. 32), they feared the people, who held that John was a prophet from God. So they answered, "We cannot tell" (v. 33). It would have been more honest had they said, "We will not tell."

6. The Parable of the Wicked Husbandmen (12:1-12). In His private instruction of His disciples Jesus spoke directly. But now that crowds were gathering around Him again "he began to speak unto them by parables" (v. 1). However, Mark records only one at this point. It is found in all three synoptic gospels.

The mention of the vineyard would remind Jesus' audience of Isaiah 5:1-7. There the *vineyard* meant "the house of Israel." Here it is probably the same. The hedge (stone fence), the winevat (winepress) and the tower (watchtower for guarding the vineyard) were all essential parts of a vineyard. The owner "let it out [rented it] to husbandmen [vinedressers]" and went abroad.

At the vintage season (Sept.—Dec.) the owner sent a servant (slave) to collect his part of the crop (v. 2). But the vinedressers took the slave, "beat him, and sent him away empty" (v. 3). When the owner sent a second slave they "wounded him in the head" (v. 4) and insulted him. A third slave "they killed, and many others" (v. 5). Finally the owner sent his son (v. 6). (*Wellbeloved* often means "only.") The vinedressers said, "Let us kill him" (v. 7) and finally did so (v. 8). The inevitable consequence would be that "the lord of the vineyard . . . will come and destroy the husbandmen, and will give the vineyard unto others" (v. 8). Jesus then quoted (vv. 10-11) from Psalm 118:22-23. He, of course, was the rejected building stone which became "the head of the corner."

The leaders of the nation "sought to lay hold on him" (v. 12), but they were afraid of the people. They recognized the fact Christ "had spoken the parable against them." They finally left Him and went away.

The meaning of the parable is rather clear. The vineyard was the Jewish nation. The vinedressers were the leaders of the nation. The slaves were the prophets, who were often mistreated. The beloved son was Christ, whom the Jewish leaders condemned to death. They would be (and were) punished in the destruction of Jerusalem by the Romans in A.D. 70. The spiritual privileges were taken away from them and given to the Gentiles.

7. The Question of Paying Taxes (12:13-17). The identity of *they* in verses 12 and 13 is not indicated. But apparently it goes back to "the chief priests, and the scribes, and the elders" of 11:27. The Sanhedrin had publicly challenged Jesus' authority and been silenced. Now it tried another tactic. It sent a delegation of Pharisees and Herodians to "catch him in his words" (v. 13)—literally, "by a word" or "in a statement." The verb for *catch*, found only here in the New Testament, meant "to catch or take by hunting or fishing." The hope was that Jesus could be trapped into making some statement that would get Him into trouble.

The insincerity of these questioners is shown in their flattering approach to Jesus: "Master [Teacher], we know that thou art true, and carest for no man: for thou regardest not the person [lit., face] of men, but teachest the way of God in truth" (v. 14). He always taught the truth! He didn't care what men thought about it, not even the Roman authorities! With this "softening up" process they hoped they had thrown

Jesus off His guard. Then they moved in quickly with their
catch question: "Is it lawful to give tribute [pay a poll tax]
to Caesar, or not?"

They thought they had Him caught on the horns of a dilem-
ma. If He said no, the Herodians would have reported Him
to the Roman authorities as a dangerous teacher who was
trying to turn the populace against the government. If He
said yes, the Pharisees would tell the people, "See, He is not
the Messiah. Instead of delivering us from foreign oppression,
He is telling us to submit to it." Whichever way He answered,
He would be in trouble.

But Jesus, "knowing their hypocrisy" (v. 15), asked for a
"penny." This was the Roman *denarius*, a silver coin (see
comment at 6:37) used for paying the poll tax. The Jews
especially hated this coin because it had on it the image of the
emperor, the reigning Tiberius, as well as his superscription,
"Tiberius Caesar, August son of the August God." To them
it was a symbol of heathen domination of God's chosen people.
The Pharisees knew that if Jesus endorsed the paying of the
poll tax He would lose the confidence of the common people.
Of course, this is what they wanted.

Turning the coin over in His hand, Jesus asked, "Whose is
this image and superscription?" They answered, "Caesar's"
(v. 16). Then He neatly walked out of their trap by making
the simple, logical statement: "Render [give back] to Caesar
the things that are Caesar's" (v. 17). In other words, "If this
coin bears Caesar's picture and name, it must belong to him.
And whatever belongs to him you should give back to him."
One can almost hear in the overtones of Jesus' voice "Why are
you carrying Caesar's picture around in your purse if you hate
him so?" And then for good measure the Master added, "and
to God the things that are God's." If the Jews had given to
God what belonged to Him, they would not now be having to

give taxes to Caesar. Erasmus made this excellent observation: "Give back to God that which has the image and superscription of God—the soul."

Someone has said of Jesus here, "He vaulted over the trap set for him, leaving them entangled in it." No wonder that "they marvelled at him."

Jesus' teaching on the question of paying taxes is perfectly clear. He taught that taxes are a debt—"give back to Caesar." We owe something to the government for the protection it gives us. The same point of view is expressed in Romans 13:7 and 1 Peter 2:13-14.

8. The Question of the Resurrection (12:18-27). Jesus had silenced the Pharisees and Herodians. Now the Sadducees (v. 18) try their hand at trapping Him. The name is supposed to have been derived from Zadok, who was high priest in the time of David. In the time of Christ the Sadducees controlled the priesthood and so had charge of the temple. In A.D. 70 the city of Jerusalem and its temple were destroyed, and the Sadducees disappeared from history.

The Sadducees, unlike the Pharisees, did not believe in any resurrection. They thought they would publicly show how ridiculous the idea of a resurrection really was. First they cited the custom of levirate marriage which Moses (v. 19) commanded, quoting Deuteronomy 25:5. If a man died childless, his brother was to marry the widow. The first male child would be legally the son and heir of the deceased father. Thus the family line would not die out.

Then the Sadducees described a hyperbolical, hypothetical case, such as probably never occurred. There were seven brethren (v. 20), who each in turn married the same woman but had no children (vv. 21-22). "In the resurrection therefore, when they shall rise [probably said sarcastically!] whose wife shall she be?" (v. 23). The Sadducees had often argued this question with the Pharisees. But now they were going to show up this untrained Galilean prophet for the ignoramus He was!

Jesus rebuked these proud, sophisticated religionists: "Do ye not therefore err [deceive yourselves], because ye know not the scriptures, neither the power of God?" (v. 24). They should have known both. Then He explained that in the next life "they neither marry, nor are given in marriage" (v. 25). Since there is no death in the new existence (Rev 21:4), there will be no need of marriage for the propagation of the human race.

The Sadducees demanded scriptural proofs for doctrines. They held primarily to the Pentateuch (the first five books of our Old Testament). So Jesus quoted from Exodus 3:6. He said, "Have ye not read in the book of Moses [the Pentateuch] how in the bush [in the passage called "The Bush," since there were no chapter and verse divisions at the time] God spake unto him, saying, I am the God of Abraham, and the God of Isaac, and the God of Jacob?" (v. 26). Then He made the application: "He is not the God of the dead, but the God of the living" (v. 27). The trouble was that the Sadducees had no vital relationship with God, just a dead ritual. The one who has experienced the resurrection power in his own life has no difficulty in believing in the resurrection of the dead.

9. The First Commandment (12:28-34). A scribe who had heard them "reasoning together" (disputing) and had seen that Jesus answered the Sadducees well, asked, "Which [lit., of what kind] is the first commandment of all?" (v. 28). The rabbis divided the 613 precepts of the law (248 commands and 365 prohibitions) into "weighty" and "light." This scribe wanted to know which command was most important.

In reply Jesus quoted the *Shema* (Deu 6:4-5) which every pious Pharisee repeated twice a day. It first emphasized the unity of Deity—"The Lord our God is one Lord" (v. 29). Then it spelled out man's chief obligation: To love God with all the heart and soul and mind and strength (v. 30)—that is, with all one's being. Jesus added, "This is the first commandment." For good measure he added a second one: "Thou shalt love thy neighbour as thyself" (v. 31). What is the most important thing in religion? Jesus said, "There is none other commandment greater than these." The apostle Paul reiterates this conclusion in Romans 13:8.

The scribe was favorably impressed: "Well, Master [Excellent, teacher!] thou hast said the truth" (v. 32). He agreed that loving God and loving one's neighbor "is more than all whole burnt offerings and sacrifices" (v. 33). This scribe showed unusual spiritual insight. "When Jesus saw that he answered discreetly [sensibly]," He gave him both an encouragement and a challenge: "Thou art not far from the kingdom of God."

10. Jesus' Question About the Son of David (12:35-37). Having silenced His inquisitors, Jesus now asked them a question: "How say the scribes that Christ [rather, the Messiah] is the son of David?" (v. 35). The words *For David himself said by the Holy Ghost* affirm both the Davidic authorship and the divine inspiration of Psalm 110 (the psalm most frequently quoted in the New Testament). In our Old Testament LORD is normally the translation of Jehovah (or Yahweh), while Lord is the rendering of Adonai. The passage here (Ps 110:1) means "The Father said to the Son." But David calls the latter *Lord* (v. 37); how can this Lord be *his son*? The answer is clear to us: Jesus was the Son of David "according to the flesh" (Ro 1:3); but He was also the Son of God, and so David's Lord. But these theologians had no answer for Christ's question. In contrast, "the common people heard him gladly."

They sensed the sincerity and divine authority with which He spoke.

11. A Warning Against the Scribes (12:38-40). In His doctrine—better, teaching—Jesus warned the common people: "Beware of the scribes" (v. 38). They "love to go [walk] in long clothing"—flowing robes were considered a sign of wealth or nobility—and to receive "salutations in the marketplaces," promenading in public places and drawing attention to themselves. They also seek "the chief seats in the synagogues (v. 39)—the front bench facing the audience—and "the uppermost rooms [chief couches] at feasts [banquets]." But with all this they "devour widow's houses, and for a pretense make long prayers" (v. 40). In those days widows depended on scribes to write their papers for them, and these pious praying men grabbed a lion's share of the property. Jesus said they would receive greater damnation—literally, more abundant judgment.

12. The Widow's Mites (12:41-44). In contrast to the Master's condemnation of the pride and hypocrisy of the wealthy scribes was His commendation of the devotion and sacrificial giving of a poor widow. Jesus sat down where He could watch people throw their money into the treasury (v. 41). This was located in the court of the women, which, it is claimed, could hold 15,000 people. The treasury consisted of thirteen large brass receptacles with trumpet-shaped mouths, designated to receive money for different purposes.

As Jesus sat there observing, He saw "many that were rich cast in much." But along came a widow who "threw in two mites, which make a farthing" (v. 42)—"two *lepta*, which is a *quadrans*." The lepton was the smallest copper coin, worth only about one-fourth of a cent. The quadrans (Roman coin) was worth half an American penny; however, its purchasing power was more. The denarius, worth about twenty cents, was a laborer's daily wage.

The Master called His disciples, to teach them a lesson. He told them that the poor widow had cast in more (v. 43) than all the rest. This was true in proportion to what she had, for she had "cast in all that she had" (v. 44). As someone has said, "The greatest gift is that which costs the giver most." Giving is measured not by how much is given but by how much is left. Another good rule is "Give until you feel it."

13. The Olivet Discourse (13:1-37). This is the only long discourse of Jesus found in all three synoptic gospels (cf. Mt 24; Lk 21). It is so named because it was given on the Mount of Olives, just outside Jerusalem. It is often referred to as "The Little Apocalypse."

As Jesus was going out of the temple one day, His disciples exclaimed over its magnificent stones and buildings (v. 1). Josephus wrote, "Now the temple was built of stones that were white and strong, and each of their length was twenty-five cubits, their height was eight, and their breadth about twelve." (A cubit equaled a foot and a half.) The buildings were also beautiful. The sanctuary is said to have been over a hundred feet high, with walls of white marble and roof gilded with gold. It was an impressive sight.

In reply Jesus made a shattering announcement: "There shall not be left one stone upon another, that shall not be thrown down" (v. 2). This prediction was fulfilled very literally in A.D. 70, when the Roman armies under Titus destroyed Jerusalem.

A little later Jesus was sitting "upon the mount of Olives over against the temple" (v. 3). The four fishermen-disciples came to Him privately with a question: "When shall these things be? And what shall be the sign when all these things shall be fulfilled?" (v. 4). The Olivet Discourse is Christ's answer to this twofold query.

The Master began with a warning: *"Take heed lest any man*

deceive you" (v. 5). He predicted that many would come in His name, saying, *I am* (v. 6)—that is, "I am He." They would hear of "wars and rumours of wars . . . but the end shall not be yet" (v. 7). In addition to international wars there would be earthquakes and famines (v. 8). These would be but the beginning of *sorrows*—literally, "birth pangs" (of a new age).

Jesus also warned His disciples that they would be delivered up to councils (v. 9)—literally, sanhedrins (in the local communities)— and beaten in synagogues. These expressions refer to the early Jewish persecution of believers. But later they would be brought before Gentile "rulers and kings . . . for a testimony against [rather, to] them." Paul was brought before many Roman rulers and gave a witness for Christ (e.g., to Agrippa).

"And the gospel must first be published among all nations" (v. 10). There was a limited fulfillment of this in the first century as the gospel spread around the Roman world. There has been a much greater fulfillment in the last two hundred years. In a very true sense one could say that the gospel has now been published to all nations, though it has not reached every tribe.

"Take no thought beforehand what ye shall speak" (v. 11) is not advice to preachers but consolation to the persecuted. The Holy Spirit would give them what to say. Verse 12 tells the sad story of cruelty between brothers, parents and children. Christ's followers will be hated by all men "for my name's sake" (v. 13). Only those who endure to the end will be saved (spiritually and eternally). Their endurance is not the basis of their salvation; rather it is the result of their new birth (Ro 8:29-39; 1 Jn 2:19, 24).

What is the *"abomination of desolation"* (lit., abomination of making desolate)? The phrase is taken from Daniel (9:27; 11:31; 12:11). The primary reference in Daniel was to the desecration of the temple by Antiochus Epiphanes in 168 B.C. There was a partial fulfillment of the prophecy here in the profaning of the temple in A.D. 70, when Jews killed each other within its sacred precincts. We look for the final fulfillment at the close of this age, when the man of lawlessness is revealed and takes his seat in the temple of God, displaying himself as God (2 Th 2:3-4).

In his parallel passage Luke (21:20) substitutes "Jerusalem compassed with armies." In obedience to the command, "let them that be in Judaea flee to the mountains," the Jewish Christians in the days leading up to the destruction of Jerusalem in A.D. 70 escaped from the Roman army and fled to Pella, east of the Jordan River. The urgency of the flight is underscored graphically in verses 15-18. They were to pray that their flight "be not in winter" (v. 18), when it would be cold and difficult to ford the flooding Jordan.

Jesus went on to say that in those days there would be affliction (better, tribulation) such as the world has never seen nor will see (v. 19). This has a striking parallel in the words of Josephus about the fall of Jerusalem in A.D. 70: "It appears to me that the misfortunes of all men, from the beginning of the world, if they be compared to these of the Jews, are not so considerable as they were." But, again, the complete fulfillment of Jesus' prediction awaits the great tribulation at the end of this age. The same goes for verse 20—first the shortness (five months) of the siege of Jerusalem in A.D. 70, and then finally the tribulation yet to come. Meanwhile there will be "false Christs and false prophets" (v. 22), but the Master has "foretold you all things" (v. 23).

Some feel that verses 14-23 deal primarily with events surrounding the destruction of Jerusalem in A.D. 70, but that verses 24-37 relate to the second coming and the end of the age. Quite clearly verses 24-27 describe the coming of the Son of

Man. (See Mt 24:27-31.) It will be preceded by startling catastrophes in nature (vv. 24-25). "And then shall they see the Son of man coming in the clouds with great power and glory" (v. 26). This is "after that tribulation" (v. 24). The angels will "gather together his elect" (v. 27) for the final, full bringing in of the kingdom.

Jesus gave "a parable [brief lesson] of the fig tree" (v. 28). When leaves appear, one knows that summer is near. So "when ye shall see these things come to pass, know that it [or, He] *is nigh*" (v. 29).

The interpretation of verse 30 has caused much comment. The most natural application would be to the generation of Jesus' day, which witnessed the destruction of Jerusalem in A.D. 70. But how does that fit in with the coming of the Son of man (v. 26)? So some have suggested taking *generation* here as meaning "race"—the Greek can mean either one. The idea would then be that the Jewish race would not pass away before all these things were fulfilled. In the light of Hitler's expressed determination to destroy all Jews, this interpretation takes on new significance. A third possible interpretation is that the generation at the close of this age that sees the beginning of these signs will live to see their final fulfillment. In any case, we have the promise: "Heaven and earth shall pass away: but my words shall not pass away" (v. 31).

The Olivet Discourse appropriately closes with admonitions to watch (vv. 32-37). This is the final value and purpose of all study of prophecy. Jesus declared that no man knows the time of His second coming, "not the angels . . . neither the Son, but the Father" (v. 32). In the light of this fact, He urges, "Take ye heed, watch and pray: for ye know not when the time is" (v. 33). When a man goes on a long journey he gives to each servant his work and commands the porter to watch (v. 34). Again Jesus urges, "Watch ye therefore" (v.

35), for we do not know at what hour our Lord might come. *Even, midnight, cockcrowing* and *morning* represent the four Roman watches of the night. We must not be found sleeping (v. 36) when He comes. This great discourse closes with the repeated admonition: "And what I say unto you I say unto all, Watch" (v. 37). That is where we must keep the emphasis in both preaching and private living.

14. The Plot Against Jesus (14:1-2). It was two days before the Passover and the feast of unleavened bread (v. 1) which immediately followed it. The chief priests and the scribes were seeking how they might seize Jesus by craftiness and put Him to death. They were afraid to do it at the feast, "lest there be an uproar of the people" (v. 2). Jesus was surrounded by thousands of Galilean pilgrims who would take His part.

15. The Anointing at Bethany (14:3-9). This is the same anointing as that recorded in Matthew 26:6-13 and John 12:2-8, but definitely not to be equated with that in Luke 7:36-50. The latter was by a sinful woman off the street in Galilee. This one was by Mary of Bethany in Judaea.

There is a chronological problem here. John places the anointing before the triumphal entry (Jn 12:1) on Friday or Saturday evening. Matthew and Mark place it on Tuesday or Wednesday evening of Passion Week. The best solution seems to be that it took place on the earlier day, but was placed later by Mark (and Matthew) because it fitted better into his narrative at that point, serving as a sharp contrast to the treacherous actions of Judas. Chronological order was not the main concern of the gospel writers.

Nothing is known about this Simon (v. 3). Probably he was a leper who had been healed by Jesus. As Christ "sat at meat [was reclining at the table]" a woman came with an alabaster container (probably a flask) "of ointment of spikenard [rather, genuine nard, an East Indian aromatic herb] very precious [costly]." Breaking off the neck of the flask, she poured the perfume on His head.

"Some . . . had indignation" (v. 4), protesting *"this waste of the ointment. . . .* it might have been sold for more than three hundred pence [denarii]" and the money "given to the poor" (v. 5). They *"murmured* [were angry] *against her."* Since a denarius was a day's wage, this would represent nearly a year's wages.

Jesus answered the objections of the guests. (John's gospel—12:4-6—indicates that Judas Iscariot was the main complainer.) He told them to let her alone, "she hath wrought a good work on me" (v. 6)—better, "she has done a beautiful thing to me." Equally significant is the statement "She hath done what she could" (v. 8). In fact she came early to anoint His body "to the burying [for the burial]." Wherever the gospel was "preached throughout the whole world" (v. 9), this incident would be told "for a memorial of her." This prediction has been fulfilled abundantly because the story is preserved in the gospels.

16. The Treachery of Judas (14:10-11). Perhaps still angry at the possible loss of money, "Judas Iscariot, one of the twelve" (v. 10) went to the chief priests to arrange Jesus' betrayal. This was the opportunity they had been waiting for. They "promised to give him money" (v. 11), which was what he wanted.

17. The Preparation for the Passover (14:12-16). It was "the first day of unleavened bread, *when they killed the passover"* (v. 12). The Passover lamb was slain in the afternoon (3:00 P.M.) of the fourteenth day of the Jewish month Nisan. The Passover meal was eaten that evening, which was the 15th of Nisan. The disciples asked where they should prepare to eat the Passover. The rabbinical ruling was that the meal must be eaten between sunset and midnight by a group of between ten and twenty people for each lamb. So Jesus and His twelve apostles made an ideal group.

In response Jesus sent two of His disciples (v. 13), Peter and John (Lk 22:8). He gave them cryptic instructions. They were to go into the city (Jerusalem) and find a man "bearing a pitcher [pottery jar] of water." It would be easy to spot him, since water jars were usually carried by women. Whenever men carried water it was in large skins.

They were to follow this man (probably a slave). Wherever he entered, they were to ask "the good man of the house [the householder]" (v. 14) for the location of the guestchamber. He would show them "a large upper room furnished and prepared" (v. 15)—that is, spread with carpets and cushions, and prepared for the meal by being furnished with a low table and with couches on which they could recline around the table. The disciples were to "make ready for us," that is, get the food for the evening meal. The two disciples went into the city, found everything as Jesus had told them, and "made ready the passover" (v. 16).

18. The Last Supper (14:17-21). That evening Jesus came with the twelve (v. 17). As they were reclining and eating, Jesus made a shattering announcement: "One of you which eateth with me shall betray me" (v. 18). Shocked and sorrowful, the disciples asked, "one by one, Is it I?" (v. 19). The Greek indicates that a negative answer is expected. A good rendering would be "Surely it is not I!"

The traitor was identified as "one of the twelve, that dippeth with me in the dish" (v. 20). This made the crime of Judas Iscariot all the more heinous. "The Son of man" (v. 21) was indeed going, "as it is written of him: but woe to that man by whom the Son of man is betrayed!" Here is the combination of divine authority and human freedom.

19. The Lord's Supper (14:22-25). As they were eating,

"Jesus took bread, and blessed, and brake it" (v. 22). Distributing it to His disciples, He said: "Take, eat: this is my body." It is obvious that the true meaning is "This *represents* my body," for the physical body of Jesus was intact before the disciples' eyes. Then the Master took the cup (v. 23) and gave thanks again. Then He passed the cup around the circle, "and they all drank [out] of it." "And he said unto them, This is [represents] my blood of the new testament, which is shed for many" (v. 24). "Covenant" is a more accurate translation than *testament*. The Jews made covenants, sometimes sealing them with blood. But the idea of a testament, or will, was foreign to the Jews until the time of the Herods.

As they finished the Lord's Supper, Jesus solemnly declared that He would not again drink "of the fruit of the vine" (v. 25) until He drank it "new in the kingdom of God." Thus the supper ended on a note of hope, looking forward to the second coming. The Master and His disciples were facing suffering and death, but one day they would be reunited forever in the kingdom.

20. Peter's Self-Confidence (14:26-31). In the Christian church the Lord's Supper replaces the Jewish Passover. It was fitting, therefore, that the Lord's Supper should be instituted in connection with the last Passover eaten by Jesus and His disciples.

At the close of the meal they sang a hymn (v. 26). This would be the latter part of the Great Hallel (praise), consisting of Psalm 115—118, which was sung at the Passover. Then they went out to the Mount of Olives.

As they walked through the cobbled streets of Jerusalem, Jesus warned His disciples that they would all "be offended" (v. 27). Probably the better translation is "All of you will stumble." The disciples stumbled over the fact that Jesus, as Messiah, did not assert His divine power in overthrowing His enemies but rather submitted to them and allowed Himself to be crucified. As Paul said (1 Co 1:23), Christ crucified is to the Jews a "stumblingblock" (same root as here). Jesus quoted from Zechariah 13:7. The Shepherd (Jesus) would be smitten, and the sheep (the disciples) would be scattered. But He would rise from the dead and see them again in Galilee (v. 28).

Peter was always outspoken. Now he asserted that although all the other disciples should stumble, "yet not I" (v. 29). Poor man, he did not know how weak he was. Jesus informed him that "this day, even in this night"—the new Jewish day had already begun at sunset—before the cock crowed *twice* (only in Mark), "thou shalt deny me thrice" (v. 30).

Instead of humbly praying, "Lord, help me!" Peter kept on asserting "the more vehemently" (v. 31) that he would die with Christ before he would deny Him. All the other disciples likewise affirmed their loyalty. They were all pathetically unaware of their inner weakness.

21. The Agony in the Garden (14:32-42). The word *Gethsemane* (v. 32) means "oil-press"; that is, a press for squeezing the oil out of olives. The Mount of Olives was so named because it was covered with olive trees. Olive oil was used for cooking, as a hairdressing, as a salve, and for fuel in the little lamps of that day.

At the entrance to this olive grove Jesus asked eight of His disciples to sit down while He went and prayed. He took with Him *"Peter and James and John"* (v. 33)—the same three who had been with Him at the raising of Jairus' daughter (5:37) and on the mount of transfiguration (9:2)—and began to be "sore [greatly] amazed, and to be very heavy [distressed]." The strong Greek words used here suggest terrified surprise and deep anguish. This is further reflected in Jesus' words: "My soul is exceeding sorrowful unto death" (v. 34). In other words, "This burden is killing me, is crushing the life out of me." He asked His three most trusted apostles to tarry and keep on watching while He prayed.

Then the Master "went forward a little, and fell on the ground" (v. 35)—literally, "was falling" under the weight of the world's sins. In agony of soul He "prayed that, if it were possible, the hour might pass from him." Earlier we are told that "his hour was not yet come" (Jn 2:4; 7:30; 8:20). But now it had come (cf. Jn 12:23, 27; 13:1; 17:1).

Abba (v. 36) is the Aramaic word for "father." In the agony of private prayer Jesus naturally used His mother tongue. He asked that the *cup* might be taken away from Him. Christ was not cringing in the face of physical death, as some cruel cynics have averred. Rather, He was dreading the moment when His Father's face would be turned away from Him, when He "who knew no sin" would be made a sin offering for us (2 Co 5:21). That was the *cup* from which He asked to be relieved. But even then He bowed His head in humble submission and said: "Nevertheless not what I will, but what thou wilt." And that must always be the prayer of those who follow Him.

Returning to the three disciples who were supposed to keep watch, Jesus found them fast asleep—sentries sleeping at their post! Using Peter's human name (sign of his weakness), Jesus asked, "Simon, sleepest thou?" (v. 37). He who had boasted that he was ready to die with Jesus could not even stand guard *one hour*. To these weak disciples the Master gave the admonition "Watch ye and pray, lest ye enter into temptation" (v. 38). Prayer is still our greatest safeguard. Christ recognized that their spirit was ready (willing), but their flesh (physical body) was weak.

A second time Jesus went away to pray "and spake the same words" (v. 39)—literally, "saying the same word," that is, "uttering the same petition." Returning to the three He once more found them asleep, "for their eyes were heavy" (v. 40) with weariness and sorrow. Ashamed and confused, they knew (wist) not what excuse to give.

When the Master returned to His three disciples the third time, He said, "Sleep on now, and take your rest" (v. 41). But this is very awkward in view of what follows in verse 42. The whole problem is solved, however, by correctly translating the above words of Jesus: "Are you still sleeping and taking your rest?" This also explains "it is enough," that is, "You have slept long enough." "The hour is come"—the hour of His betrayal, trial and crucifixion. They must rise up and go (v. 42), for the betrayer was approaching.

22. The Arrest of Jesus (14:43-52). Even as Jesus was saying these words, Judas arrived. He was "one of the twelve" (v. 43), which made his crime all the more heinous. With him was a crowd of men with swords and clubs, sent by the chief priests and the scribes and the elders, that is, the Sanhedrin. The betrayer had given his followers *a token* (v. 44)—or, "a signal" (lit., a sign agreed upon). The one whom he kissed was their victim. They were to take (seize) Him and "lead him away safely." Judas was taking no chances on Jesus being rescued by His disciples.

Immediately coming to Jesus, Judas greeted Him as Master (rabbi)—the best Greek text has it only once—and *kissed* Him. The compound verb used here is defined by J. H. Thayer as meaning "to kiss much, kiss again and again, kiss tenderly." This makes Judas' act doubly diabolical. After the betrayer had performed his deed, his companions laid their hands on Jesus and took (seized) Him.

"One of them that stood by" (v. 47) is identified as Peter in John 18:10. True to his promise to stand by his Master, he drew his sword and cut off the ear of a servant of the high priest. Probably Peter swung his sword to take off the servant's head, but the man ducked and lost only his ear. If the gospel of Mark was written while Peter was still alive, it can easily be understood why his name is not given here.

Christ remonstrated with His captors. Had they come out "as against a thief [robber], with swords and with staves [clubs]" (v. 48) to seize Him? Why had they not arrested Him while He was teaching daily in the temple? But all this had happened in order that the scriptures might be fulfilled (v. 49). The reference is probably to Isaiah 53. And as Jesus had predicted, "they all forsook him, and fled" (v. 50).

Verse 51 and 52 form an intriguing footnote to the betrayal scene. The "certain young man" is, without much doubt, John Mark, the author of this gospel. If the Last Supper took place in the home of his mother (cf. Ac 12:12), it is easy to reconstruct the incident. Judas Iscariot, having left the upper room between the Last Supper and Lord's Supper, naturally returned there with his mob to seize Jesus. Finding that the Master had left, he proceeded to the familiar haunt on the slopes of the Mount of Olives (Jn 18:2). Wakened by all the excitement, young John Mark threw a linen cloth over his body and ran to the garden to warn Jesus but arrived just too late. When one of the crowd grabbed his shoulder, he slid out of the cloth and rushed home. These verses are his way of saying, "I was there."

23. The Trial Before Caiaphas (14:53-65). His captors led Jesus away to the high priest's house, where the Sanhedrin had assembled (v. 53). Peter "followed him afar off" (v. 54) into the palace (courtyard) of the high priest. In Jerusalem (approximately 2,500 feet above sea level) the nights are cold in the early spring. So Peter sat with the servants, warming himself at a fire.

The chief priests (v. 55) took the lead in trying Jesus. In

Galilee it had been the Pharisees who opposed Him. But when He cleansed the temple (11:15-18), He threatened both the power and the pocketbooks of the chief priests. From then on they were determined to destroy Him. So they with the "council [Sanhedrin] sought for witness against Jesus to put him to death." But they found none. There were many false witnesses (v. 56), but they could not agree in their testimony. Certain (v. 57) of them did try to trump up the false charge that He had said He would "destroy this temple . . . and within three days . . . build another" (v. 58). This was apparently a garbled echo of the saying recorded in John 2:19: "Destroy this temple, and in three days I will raise it up." But even here the witnesses could not agree together (v. 59) as to what Jesus had said.

Frustrated, the high priest demanded, "Answerest thou nothing?" (v. 60). He hoped that Christ would incriminate Himself by making some unwise statement. But Jesus "held his peace" (v. 61). So now Caiaphas asked Him a direct question: "Art thou the Christ [the Messiah], the Son of the Blessed?" (The Jews feel it is not reverent to refer directly to God; so they use such euphemistic substitutes as "the Blessed.") In reply Jesus gave a direct answer: *I am* (v. 62)—perhaps consciously echoing the name of God told to Moses at the burning bush (Ex 3:14). He added that they would see the Son of man sitting on the right hand of *power*—another euphemism for God—"and coming in the clouds of heaven" (cf. Dan 7:13; Ps 110:1). Someday the members of the Sanhedrin would be on trial before Jesus.

The reaction of Caiaphas was drastic. He "rent his clothes" (v. 63). Though the Law forbade the high priest to tear his garments as a sign of personal grief (Lev 10:6; 21:10), the rabbis later prescribed this act in the case of hearing blasphemy. Caiaphas now declared that they needed no further

witnesses, for they had all heard Jesus' *blasphemy* (v. 64).
On the basis of this the Sanhedrin condemned Christ as guilty
of death, though they were not permitted by the Roman government to carry out the death penalty. But they took out
their spite by spitting on Him. Blindfolding Him, they struck
His face, challenging Him to prophesy (v. 65) who it was who
hit Him (cf. Mt 26:68). The attendants "received Him with
blows" (best Greek text). This was the way sinful men treated
the sinless Son of God.

24. Peter's Denials (14:66-72). Peter's seeking bodily comfort near the fire got him into trouble. One of the maids of the
high priest saw him in the *palace* (v. 66)—rather, the courtyard around which the palace was built. As the light of the
fire played on Peter's face, she "looked upon him" (v. 67)
intently and exclaimed, "You also were with the Nazarene,
Jesus." Probably she had seen the apostle with his Master in
the streets of Jerusalem.

Caught in a trap, Peter denied (v. 68) his Lord. Impulsively
he answered, "I neither know nor understand what you are
saying." To escape further detection he went out into the
porch (vestibule). But *the* maid (so the best Greek text)
spotted him and began again to say to those standing by, "This
is one of them" (v. 69). Once more he denied it (v. 70). A
little later those standing nearby joined in on the accusation.
They recognized him as a Galilean by his accent.

Then Peter began "to curse and to swear" (v. 71), asserting
that he did not know the man about whom they were speaking.
The translation here may be misleading. It does not refer to
what we now commonly call "cursing and swearing." The first
verb simply means that he was saying, "Let me be under a
curse if I am not telling you the truth." The second verb means
to swear an oath, as one does in court.

About this time the cock crowed "the second time" (v. 72).
At last Peter came to his senses. He recalled Jesus' prediction

that before the cock crowed twice he would deny Him thrice. Stabbed with conviction and remorse, he went out into the night and *wept*. The Greek words of the last sentence are difficult to translate, but probably they mean that he broke down and kept on weeping.

25. The Trial Before Pilate (15:1-5). The night meeting of the Sanhedrin was illegal, at least according to later rabbinical rules. So as soon as morning came, an official session was convened. From that Jesus was led bound (v. 1) to *Pilate*. This was Pontius Pilate, governor of Judea (A.D. 26-36). The first inscription bearing his name was found as recently as 1961, in excavations at ancient Caesarea on the seacoast. Ordinarily Pilate would have been residing there in the official Roman palace. But at the Passover season, when religious riots often took place, the governor found it wise to be in Jerusalem with extra contingents of soldiers.

When Pilate saw Jesus in the humble dress of a Galilean, he asked, probably contemptuously, "You! Are You the king of the Jews?" Christ's reply was, "Thou sayest it" (v. 2)—literally, "You are saying." This can be taken in either of two ways. It may be an emphatic affirmative answer, similar to our slang expression, "You said it!" Or it may be noncommittal: "It is you that say that, not I." In this case we would say that Jesus purposely gave an ambiguous answer because Pilate's concept of "king of the Jews" was that of a political ruler in opposition to the Roman government. Jesus was *the King of the Jews,* but His was a spiritual kingdom.

The chief priests were accusing Him of many things (v. 3). Finally Pilate, perplexed at Jesus' silence, said, "Answerest thou nothing?" (v. 4). Still Christ stood there with perfect poise and answered nothing (v. 5), in fulfillment of Isaiah 53:7. No wonder that Pilate marveled!

26. The Choice of Barabbas (15:6-15). At the Passover feast

Pilate ordinarily released to the Jews one prisoner (v. 6), whichever one they begged for. It happened that there was a notorious prisoner named Barabbas (v. 7, Mt 27:16). He had made insurrection against Rome, and in the revolt had committed murder. In the eyes of the emperor he would be considered a dangerous political prisoner.

When the people began to clamor for the usual release (v. 8), Pilate thought he saw a way to get rid of Jesus without deciding His case. He asked if they wished him to release to them "the King of the Jews" (v. 9). He knew that it was because of envy (v. 10) that the chief priests had delivered Jesus to him. Fearful that they might now lose their prey, "the chief priests moved [stirred up] the people" (v. 11) to ask for Barabbas instead.

Once more Pilate tried to free Jesus. He asked what he should do with the one they called the King of the Jews (v. 12). Urged on by the chief priests, the people now yelled out, "Crucify him" (v. 13). For the last time Pilate pleaded the case of the man he knew to be innocent (cf. Lk 23:4; Jn 18:38). He asked, "Why, what evil hath he done?" (v. 14). But this mob, like all mobs, was in no mood for reasoning. "More exceedingly" they yelled loudly, "Crucify him." Pilate, "willing to content the people, released Barabbas unto them" (v. 15) and in doing so committed a major crime against the empire. His desire to satisfy the people did him no good. Because of his cruel administration he was later recalled to Rome. He lost all the way around.

Pilate scourged Jesus. Prisoners sometimes died under this terrible ordeal. A short whip of leather strips, with pieces of metal and bone attached to them, was brought down over the victim's back. Jesus survived and was handed over to be crucified.

27. The Soldiers' Mockery of Jesus (15:16-20). The Roman soldiers led Jesus "into the hall" (v. 16)—rather, "inside the courtyard." It was called by a Latin name, *Praetorium,* and signified the governor's official residence. The location of this in Jerusalem is debated. Some think it was Herod's palace, near the present Jaffa Gate in the west wall. Others hold that it was the Tower of Antonia, at the northwest corner of the temple area on the east side of the city. The latter is the traditional site pointed out today, because of the discovery there of a large paved area (cf. Jn 19:13) which may have been the courtyard.

The soldiers called together the whole band. This was a tenth of a Roman legion and so ordinarily consisted of about six hundred men. But the reference here may be to some soldiers who happened to be hanging around at the time. These put on Jesus a purple robe and on His head a crown of thorns (v. 17), mocking symbols of royalty. Then they saluted Him with "Hail, King of the Jews" (v. 18). Cruelly they smote (v. 19) Him on the head, probably driving the sharp thorns into His brow. Repeatedly they were spitting on Him. To add insult to injury, the soldiers, "bowing their knees, worshipped him," that is, did homage. The whole scene is revolting in its cruelty. When they had given vent to their feelings, they led Him out to crucify Him (v. 20).

28. The Crucifixion (15:21-41). Apparently Jesus was so weak that He was unable to carry His cross. This is not surprising, after the scourging He had received. So the soldiers "compel [impress into service] Simon a Cyrenian" (v. 21) to carry the cross. He was coming out of the country to the city. He is further identified as the "father of Alexander and Rufus." Mark is supposed to have written his gospel at Rome, and these two brothers may have been well-known members of the church there. Rufus is referred to in Romans 16:13.

The soldiers brought Jesus to "the place Golgotha" (v. 22),

an Aramaic word meaning "skull." The term *Calvary*, which occurs only once in the King James Version of the Bible (Lk 23:33), is from the Latin word for skull, *calvaria*, occurring in the Vulgate Version of all four gospels. The location of Calvary is still a matter of dispute. The traditional site is in the Church of the Holy Sepulcher, which is west of the temple area. But many Protestants prefer Gordon's Calvary, outside of the north wall of Jerusalem.

Those who crucified Jesus offered Him "wine mingled with myrrh" (v. 23). This was evidently provided by the women of Jerusalem for condemned criminals, in order to deaden their pain. Jesus refused to take this drug (see 14:25), apparently because He wanted to keep His mind clear. The soldiers gambled over His garments, "casting lots" (v. 24) to ascertain what each should take.

The time of the crucifixion was "the third hour" (v. 25)— nine o'clock in the morning. Over Jesus' head was placed the "superscription" (v. 26), indicating the accusation, or charge, against Him. The exact wording of the inscription is slightly different in the four gospels, but there is no contradiction. Mark has the shortest form: THE KING OF THE JEWS.

With Jesus were crucified two thieves (v. 27)—rather, "two robbers." A robber is one who takes by force. These two robbers, one on each side of Christ, were probably associated with Barabbas in his revolution. It is rather evident that Barabbas was destined for the middle cross; but Jesus died in his place. The scene was a fulfillment of the scripture (v. 28) found in Isaiah 53:12.

The mockery of the Jews was doubtless more painful to Jesus than that of the pagan soldiers. Those who passed by "railed on him" (v. 29)—literally, "were blaspheming him." Echoing the words of the false witnesses before the Sanhedrin, they taunted Him as the one who was going to destroy the temple and build it in three days. Then they challenged Him: "Save thyself, and come down from the cross" (v. 30). The chief priests and scribes (v. 31) were the worst offenders. Speaking better than they knew, they said, "He saved others; himself he cannot save." The truth was that had He saved Himself He could not have saved others. They challenged "Christ the King of Israel" (v. 32) to come down from the cross, "that we may see and believe." But they had rejected the many miracles He had already performed. They did not need to see more; what they needed was a change of attitude. Even the two robbers crucified with Jesus reviled Him. But one later repented and found forgiveness (Lk 23:39-43).

From the sixth hour (noon) until the ninth hour (3:00 P.M.) there was darkness over the whole land (v. 33)—probably meaning Palestine. Since the Passover always came at the time of the full moon, this could not have been an eclipse of the sun. It is likely that the sky was covered with very heavy black clouds as a symbol of God's judgment on sin.

But this darkness over the land was more than matched by the black night that settled over Jesus' spirit. At three o'clock He cried out in Aramaic, "My God, my God, why hast thou forsaken me?" (v. 34)—a quotation from Psalm 22:1. This is the wail of a lost soul. It was God's will that His Son should "taste death for every man" (Heb 2:9). This was not only physical death but spiritual death. It would seem that in the human consciousness of Jesus He felt at this moment as though He were lost. This is the price He had to pay to redeem us.

When some of the bystanders heard Jesus crying out *Eloi, Eloi,* they said (perhaps in heartless mockery) that He was calling "Elias" (v. 35)—Elijah. Someone, probably a soldier, filled a sponge with vinegar (v. 36)—the "sour wine" which was the common drink of laborers and soldiers—and offered the soaked sponge to Jesus. The meaning of *let alone* is not clear. Apparently it means, "Let me alone"; that is, "Do not stop me from giving it to Him." Matthew 27:49 has "the rest" saying, "Let be"; that is, "Let him alone." Perhaps the saying in Matthew came first, then that in Mark. The last clause of verse 36 would then mean, "Let me give him this and then see whether Elijah comes to help him."

At this juncture Jesus uttered a loud cry and "gave up the ghost" (v. 37)—literally, "breathed out", or "expired." As he did so, "the veil of the temple" (v. 38)—the inner veil of the sanctuary, in front of the holy of holies—was rent in two "from the top to the bottom." Thus the beautiful, intricately woven tapestry was not ripped by human hands, but by a divine miracle. The significance of this event is indicated in Hebrews 10:19-22. It symbolized the fact that the way was now opened through Christ's death for all His followers to enter the very presence of God at all times.

Standing near the cross was the centurion (v. 39) who was in charge of the crucifixion (cf. v. 44). When he witnessed the way in which Jesus died, he said, "Truly this man was the Son of God." In the Greek there is no article before *Son;* so it could be translated "a son of God," that is, "a godly man." That is the way Luke interpreted it for his Greek readers. He has the centurion saying, "Certainly this was a righteous man" (Lk 23:47). If we believe in the inspiration of Luke's gospel as well as Mark's, it would seem that this is the interpretation we should accept.

Besides the callous Roman soldiers, the cruel Jewish mockers, and the serious-minded centurion, there was another important group at the cross. It was composed of "women looking on afar off" (v. 40). Three are named. One was Mary Magdalene, from the town of Magdala on the west shore of the Lake of Galilee. Another Mary was the mother of James the less—so called because he was shorter in stature, younger in age, or less important among the apostles. Salome seems to have been the wife of Zebedee (cf. Mt 27:56). These women had attended to Jesus' material needs during His ministry in Galilee (v. 41). They were the last to leave the cross and the first to come to the tomb on Sunday morning (cf. 16:1). There were also many other women who followed Jesus to Jerusalem.

29. The Burial of Jesus (15:42-47). The *even* referred to here (v. 42) was evidently what was sometimes called "the first evening," from three o'clock until sunset. The *preparation* is defined as being "the day before the sabbath." Since Jesus died at about three o'clock in the afternoon and no burial could take place on the Sabbath, which began at sunset, there was no time to be lost. "Joseph of Arimathaea, an honourable counsellor" (v. 43)—a member of the Sanhedrin—was, like Nicodemus, a secret disciple of Jesus (Jn 19:38). He went in boldly to Pilate and *craved* (asked for) the body of Jesus.

The governor "marvelled [wondered] if he were already dead" (v. 44). Ordinarily, crucified criminals hung for at least a day or two on the cross before they expired. So Pilate summoned the centurion who was in charge of the crucifixion and asked if Jesus had died. When the officer answered in the affirmative, the governor "gave the body to Joseph" (v. 45). The devout councilor bought fine linen (v. 46). Tenderly taking the body of Christ from the cross, he wrapped it in the fine linen and laid it in "a sepulchre which was hewn out of a rock." Such tombs were common in that day. Watching the burial were Mary Magdalene and Mary the mother of Joses (v. 47), who have already been mentioned in verse 40.

V

THE RESURRECTION
(16:1-20)

1. The Women at the Empty Tomb (16:1-8). When the Sabbath (v. 1) ended at sunset on Saturday the same three women that were named in 15:40 as watching Jesus' death brought sweet spices that they might anoint the body of Jesus in the tomb. "Very early in the morning of the first day of the week" (v. 2) they came to the sepulcher at sunrise.

As they approached, they were asking each other, "Who shall roll us away the stone from the door of the sepulchre?" (v. 3). We are told that it was "very great" (v. 4), evidently too heavy for them to move. But to their joy they discovered that it had already been rolled back from the entrance. Entering the tomb, they saw "a young man . . . clothed in a long white garment" (v. 5). Naturally they were thoroughly frightened at the sight of the angel. But he quickly quieted their fears with the words "Be not affrighted." The rest of verse 6 reads literally, "Jesus you seek, the Nazarene, the one who has been crucified? He rose! He is not here! See the place where they laid him." The angel then told them to go and tell Jesus' disciples *and Peter* (v. 7)—this comforting item is found only in Mark—that their Master would meet them in Galilee, as He had told them (cf. 14:28). The women "fled from the sepulchre" (v. 8) with trembling and astonishment. At first they told no one what they had seen or heard, for they were afraid.

125

All four gospels end with the climactic event of the resurrection. This was the proof that Jesus was the Messiah, the Saviour of the world. His resurrection validated His atoning death and is the basis of our justification (Ro 4:25).

2. Various Appearances of Jesus (16:9-20). These last twelve verses of Mark are not found in the two oldest Greek manuscripts of the New Testament, Vaticanus and Sinaiticus (fourth century). Eusebius, writing in the same century, says that they were lacking "in almost all the existent copies of the Gospel . . . the accurate ones at all events." Jerome (about A.D. 400) says that they were found "in few Gospels" and were missing in "almost all the Greek copies." The earliest known commentary on Mark (sixth century) stops at 16:8. It is almost universally agreed that verses 9-20 were added centuries after the gospel was written, in order to complete it with a summary account of the postresurrection appearances of Jesus.

The appearance to Mary Magdalene (v. 9) is described at length in John 20:1-18. The disclosure to "two of them" (v. 12) is related in full in Luke 24:13-35. The appearance to "the eleven" (v. 14) is given in John 20:24-29. The Great Commission (v. 15) is found in fuller form in Matthew 28:18-20.

The appendix (vv. 9-20) ends with a statement of Jesus' ascension (v. 19). This is described in Luke 24:50-51 and Acts 1:9-11. The theological affirmation that He sat on the right hand of God is an echo of Romans 8:34; Ephesians 1:20; Colossians 3:1; Hebrews 1:3; 10:12-13; 12:2; and 1 Peter 3:22. This is the faith which the disciples went forth to proclaim (v. 20).

BIBLIOGRAPHY

Alexander, Joseph Addison. *Commentary on the Gospel of Mark.* Reprint. Grand Rapids: Zondervan.

Barclay, William. *The Gospel of Mark.* The Daily Study Bible. Philadelphia: Westminster, 1954.

Branscomb, B. Harvie. *The Gospel of Mark.* The Moffatt New Testament Commentary. New York: Harper, n.d.

Cole, R. A. *The Gospel According to St. Mark.* The Tyndale New Testament Commentaries. Grand Rapids: Eerdmans, 1961.

Erdman, Charles R. *The Gospel of Mark.* Philadelphia: Westminster, 1917.

Hunter, Archibald M. *The Gospel According to Saint Mark.* Torch Bible Commentaries. London: SCM, 1948.

Lenski, R. C. H. *The Interpretation of St. Mark's Gospel.* Columbus, Ohio: Wartburg, 1946.

Minear, Paul S. *The Gospel According to Mark.* The Layman's Bible Commentary. Richmond, Virginia: John Knox Press, 1962.

Mitton, C. Leslie. *The Gospel According to St. Mark.* Epworth Preacher's Commentaries. London: Epworth, 1957.

Morison, James. *A Practical Commentary on the Gospel According to St. Mark.* 6th ed. London: Hodder and Stoughton, 1889.

Moule, C. F. D. *The Gospel According to Mark.* The Cambridge Bible Commentary. Cambridge: University, 1965.

Rawlinson, A. E. J. *St. Mark.* Westminster Commentaries. London: Methuen, 1925.